BUILD YOUR
FOUNDATION

JOHN W. CARVER III

BUILD YOUR FOUNDATION

68

BUILDING BLOCKS
for a **SUCCESSFUL,**
REWARDING LIFE

Build Your Foundation
68 Building Blocks for a Successful, Rewarding Life

Published by:
Tremendous Life Books
118 West Allen Street
Mechanicsburg, PA 17055

717-766-9499   800-233-2665
Fax: 717-766-6565

www.TremendousLifeBooks.com

ISBN: 978-1-936354-42-9

Author photo by The Image Facktory Groupe:
www.TIFGroupe.com

Table of Contents

Introduction

The chapters in this book came about as I helped thousands of people, from all walks of life, who had no hope and no direction. The people I met lived life day-to-day with no long-term plans as if they were happy watching life fly right past them. I wanted to give them a road map to reach their own goals, to overcome discouragement, and to teach the secrets that can help them climb from being average and ordinary to being extraordinary. I took some bits of that road map and turned them into this book, a collection of short, easy-to-read pieces that can help you to build the foundation for a rich, successful, and rewarding life. If you have any desire to lead an extraordinary life then the words between these covers will give you "gasoline for your engine" to reach levels of success that few have achieved!

1

What's In Your Foundation?

On July 4th we celebrate America's birthday. The foundation of the United States was built on *freedom* and *individual liberty*. Every structure known to mankind has a foundation. For thousands of years people have been designing buildings for a variety of reasons. One thing that is consistent with most of the designers is their careful attention to the foundation of their structures. They understand that without solid foundations their creations will not stand.

We see in Rome, Greece, China, South America, Russia, Great Britain, and other locations, that there are structures that have stood for hundreds and thousands of years. Part of the reason they have stood so long is the foundation on which the structures stand. What's the personal equivalent in our daily lives? What are the foundations upon which we build our families and careers? Some build their lives on facts; others build upon emotions. Emotions come and go like the wind! Building a life on emotions is like building a tower on sandy soil. A life built upon facts can withstand the buffets of time and crisis.

What if the current state of your life is shaky due to some emotional decision making in the past? You certainly can't turn back the clock, but you can shore up your mental, emotional, and spiritual foundations from this day onward!

2

Contentment is Destroyed…

Here's a quote I came across a few years ago: "Contentment is destroyed by comparison." What does that mean? Here's a little story that illustrates the point:

"Little Johnny's mother places a large piece of chocolate cake on his plate. He's pretty happy with it—until he glances over at his brother's portion and notices that it's even bigger! Suddenly Johnny is no longer satisfied with what he got. He starts to pout and complain, and may even resort to throwing his cake on the floor."

It's hard for some of us to be satisfied with our own "toys" (gifts, talents and blessings). When I was growing up in the '70s

I had a friend who always wore the best shoes. When he outgrew them he would give them to me. There was a problem... my feet were always smaller than his feet. That didn't stop me. I stuffed socks in the ends of the shoes so my feet would fit. I was no longer happy with my own shoes. I wanted those fancy Florsheim boots!

Years later a close friend bought a Honda Civic. I envied that car for months. One day, while my wife was at work, I went to a dealer and was ready to buy one exactly like it. Just before I signed the paperwork I called my wife and told what I was about to do. I'll never forget her response. In her sweetest voice she said, "If that's what you want to do then do it." I knew right there I was in deep weeds. I walked out of the dealership and never did get that luxurious Honda Civic.

When we compare ourselves to others we usually come to one of three conclusions:

1. We're better than they are.

2. They're better than we are.

3. We'd rather be them than us.

It took me several years to "get" that I was born with certain talents and skill sets that were unique to me and that when I tried to be like other people I was short-changing myself and my self-worth.

Each of us was born with latent gifts and talents that need to be developed. There is a building in almost every ZIP code called a library that is loaded with free information that can help us discover why we were born and what potential resides in us. Libraries have the keys to our future; they hold a treasure of knowledge that can ignite our lives in ways we cannot imagine. Reading about people like Brian Tracy, Dale Carnegie, Mark

Sanborn, Jim Rohn, Charlie "Tremendous" Jones, Denis Waitley, and so many others can transform our lives.

There is no better you than you. Stop trying to be someone that you're not. One of the most important days in your life is when you find out *why* you were born. This is transformational. Once you identify your *why*, you'll jump out of bed every day determined to achieve your *what!*

This concept changed my life and continues to pull me toward bigger and bigger opportunities. Do not fear the future, and do not worry about keeping up with others around you. Be you. Identify *why* you were born and start living your dreams instead of someone else's.

3

Do You Know Your *Why?*

This question transformed my life! People so often get bogged down in *what* they are going to do with their lives and *how* they are going to do it, but very few people have thought about *why* they're doing it!

Dr. Alejandra Carrasco says, "The Japanese concept of ikigai roughly translates to *why I wake up in the morning.* Everyone, according to the Japanese, has an ikigai." I have visited with thousands of people and found out something remarkable: those with a huge *why* tend to accomplish great things in life.

When people identify *why* they want or need to do something, and the *why* is huge, it enables them to do *what* they're planning to do and it takes on a new purpose...a new passion. Let me give you some examples. After trying for nine years to have children, my wife and I decided to adopt. Our *why* was to make a difference in the lives of children who had no home and no family. Our *why* identified *what* we were going to do and then enabled us to figure out *how* to get it done.

Your *why* must be bigger than your *what* if you want to be able to overcome the obstacles that will try to stop you on your journey. Your *why* gets you out of bed in the morning, your *why* enables you to look discouragement in the face and keep right on going, your *why* forces you to keep moving forward when others advise you to quit.

"We create ideas that inspire enduring belief." This is the slogan of Saatchi and Saatchi, the advertising firm responsible for such well-known brands as Frosted Flakes Cereal and Heinz Ketchup. CEO Kevin Roberts said, "You feel the world through your five senses...the brands that can move to that emotional level can create loyalty BEYOND REASON...!" *Why* are they doing this? To create consumers who cannot imagine using any other product.

Again, *why* you are pursuing something must be bigger than *what* you are pursuing in order for you to make it through the dark times. Orison Swett Marden said, "There's no greater sight in the world than that of a person fired with a great purpose, dominated by one unwavering aim."

In the 1929 Rose Bowl game between California and Georgia Tech, Roy Riegels recovered a fumble for California, became disoriented, and ran toward his own end zone! Tackled by one of his own teammates at the 2-yard line, Roy's mishap enabled Georgia Tech to score a safety.

Back in the locker room at half-time, Riegels lamented, "I can't do it, Coach. I can't play. I ruined the team." The coach replied, "Get up, Riegels. The game is only half over. You belong on the field."

Sometimes you just need someone to give you a *why* that's big enough to get you moving!

4

Remember
Their Lessons

I've been playing the piano and organ since I was in my early teens. There are many people who inspired me to get better and better. Cornel taught me that excellence takes time. Barbara taught me to never lose focus. Jean taught me that you can make beautiful music wherever you are at any time. Larry, a drummer, taught me to "let loose" a little bit. Phyllis taught me that if I didn't practice I wouldn't realize excellence.

We all have teachers who have given us a little shove from time to time. Mr. Fowler, my fourth-grade teacher, taught me the difference between listening and hearing. I have never forgotten that lesson. Mr. Alsop, my seventh-grade social studies teacher, let me see the world beyond my ZIP code. Mrs. Pringle taught me how to treat shy people.

Each and every one of us has people in our lives who have made contributions. Some may have given you some encouragement when you thought you couldn't make it. Others may have said one thing that changed your life forever. Their lessons came from their experiences and they chose to share them with you and me.

You have learned some lessons in your life as well. What are you doing with the wisdom that you gained? Are you keeping it inside or are you leveraging it for other people? I will never forget the phone call I received from Terry back in 1997. My wife and I were in our ninth year of infertility. Terry heard that we were considering adopting. She is an adoptive mom so she reached out to us and made a huge difference in our lives. She shared her journey with us and now, after my wife and I have adopted six children, we share the lessons we have learned with other people.

Don't sit on your lessons. They are valuable to other people who are struggling in their own lives. Make a difference. Let them stand on your shoulders as I am standing on the shoulders of so many people in my life.

5

My Fight with Fear

Those who know me well know that I have stuttered my whole life. In fact, I cannot remember a time when I haven't stuttered. I can remember being teased and harassed almost daily because of my speech problems. I was terrified to speak. My vocal chords would freeze up. I wished and prayed for a life of fluency...to be like everyone else who didn't have to think about HOW they were going to speak. It was torture every single day.

In my sophomore year of high school I started going to vocational training for a half a day to study photography. I thought, "I love taking pictures and being a photographer would enable me to not have to talk to people all that much!" Eventually, I got a job in retail at a photography company helping customers make decisions about cameras, shooting pictures, etc. I HAD to talk to people! This was not what I had in mind for a photography career. I would often stutter, but most of the people genuinely appreciated my expertise and didn't tease me. It was refreshing!

In 1988, just after I married my wife, Tammy, my uncle, who had been in the insurance business for thirty years, suggested that I consider a career in his field. I thought he was nuts! In the insurance business I had to talk to a lot of people, be proactive about it, and face my terror of being teased and of having my vocal chords lock up. After much encouragement from my wife, I bit the bullet, passed the insurance exam, and spent the next twenty-plus years helping thousands of people (along with the hundreds of people I hired to do the same) with their insurance and retirement-planning needs. During those years I was teased, laughed at, spit upon, attacked, cursed, hit, visited homes with dog crap all over the floor, subjected to flea infestations, mice, and much more. One thing I knew, though: I was helping people.

My speech issues have gotten much better. I've given more than 540 speeches and in August 2011 I started a radio show. Is it scary? Yes! But I know that I have information that can transform people's lives if I get my focus off of me and onto other people.

Fear has a way of keeping us in the dark. Fear kept my dreams small. Fear keeps us from realizing our dreams and goals. Your fears might not be the same as mine but they are just as real. I face my fear every single time I open my mouth. You can overcome your fears as well. Eleanor Roosevelt said, "You must do the thing you think you cannot do."

Change your beliefs—and you change your behaviors.

Change your behaviors—and you change your results.

Change your results—and you change your life.

Stop letting your fear handicap you. Face it head on…push through it and watch your life blossom in ways you cannot imagine. With determination, you can climb any mountain, overcome any situation, and stare down any fear.

6

L.I.S.O.R.

In 1988 I was hired as an insurance agent with Sun Life Insurance Company of America. I was twenty one years old and they gave me one of the roughest territories on the map. It seemed that every household I visited was hostile to the very concept of life insurance. I was having a terrible time. One day I asked my sales manager for some advice and he said, "John, L.I.S.O.R." I said, "What the heck is that?" He said that it stood for:

Lacking

In

Sense

Or

Reason

I got it right away. There are people who, no matter what you teach them or how you coach them, just don't get it. This is one of the most frustrating feelings imaginable. I know that the information I am sharing can change someone's life. I give them proof so it's not just my word against theirs, but they still choose to follow a path that is not good for them. Admittedly, I've found myself on the other side of this equation as well. How about you?

One of the major keys to success is to have a "teachable point of view." *This is essential!* If you (or I) think we know everything then we do not have a "teachable point of view." This is how former CEO Jack Welch rebuilt General Electric. He taught his executives to promote a mindset of "conscious incompetence." That is, to *not* be afraid of admitting that they didn't know certain information or, put another way, "knowing that you don't know" and not allowing your ego to stand in the way of learning new information.

Seth Godin writes, "The reason coachability is so crucial is that without it, you don't have the emotional maturity to consider whether the advice is good or not. You reject the process out of hand, and end up stuck."

When we come across as a "know it all" we limit our future successes dramatically! Instead, be a sponge. Learn all you can from anybody, anywhere and at any time. Don't be like those who L.I.S.O.R. For those who are L.I.S.O.R there is only so much you can do until they come to terms with the fact that they still have much to learn.

7

Public Servants

On November 6, 2012 The United States of America voted for a President. It got me thinking about the title *Public Servant.* Most of us associate the term with paid government employees. I believe all of us should be public servants. Think of the phrase *My Pleasure!* These are the words spoken by almost everyone I have encountered who works at Chick-fil-A restaurants. Their goal is to serve. That speaks to me.

Zig Ziglar said, "You are the only person on earth who can use your ability." There was a custom in the ancient Middle East that when you entered a person's home they would wash your feet of the dust and dirt from your journey. The homeowner took on the role of a servant to those who entered. One of the biggest roadblocks to becoming a true public servant is self-centeredness. When we are mostly concerned about ourselves there leaves little room to care about other people. Another obstacle that gets in the way is perfectionism. Many believe they have to be perfect in order to be effective. This is not true!

People right in our own neighborhoods and cities are waiting for those who have "Servant Mindsets" or, as Tony Alessandra puts it, people who use "The Platinum Rule." He says, "Treat others the way they want to be treated." Aha! What a difference. The Platinum Rule accommodates the feelings of others. The focus of relationships shifts from "this is what I want, so I'll give everyone the same thing" to "let me first understand what they want and then I'll give it to them."

8

"It All Comes Out"

Someone once wrote, "Your actions show what your heart is made of." How many times have you seen someone respond to a situation in a way that shocked you? Maybe they exploded into a rage, "wrote you off" for a simple mistake, or put you down so much you didn't think you could take another step forward.

I believe there are more people suffering at the hands and mouths of those they trusted than most of us can comprehend. Philip Yancey once said, "You cannot suddenly fabricate foundations of strength. They must have been building all along." The overwhelming majority base their opinions of themselves on *other people's opinions* of them. So many of them forget that the opinions of others are not necessarily facts!

Here are some ways for you to build *Foundations of Strength* in your own life so the outbursts and painful words and actions of others do not slow you down:

Write your goals on paper DAILY.

Read or listen to a book a month that can pull you toward where you want to go. Become a life-long student.

Learn to say no to requests that distract you from your goals!

Forgive yourself of your mistakes…and seek forgiveness from those *you* hurt.

Fire those in your life who don't encourage you to move forward.

Always tell the truth!

Walk upright (don't slouch).

Give to others who have no way of paying you back.

Stay away from negative people.

Surround yourself with people who believe in you!

These habits will help you build those foundations of strength that will enable you to see —and go! —farther than you can possibly imagine.

Anyone can be a Public Servant. Look for ways to serve and realize the intense joy and fulfillment you will receive when you do things for people who have no way of paying you back.

9

She's on the Edge!

On April 16, 2013 Tammy and I celebrated our 25th wedding anniversary. It's hard to believe it's been twenty-five years. She is my best friend! We decided to go to Arizona for our honeymoon and, thanks to my parents, we were able to go. I had traveled to Arizona as a kid along with my family many times. My new wife had never been "out west" so I thought it would be nice for her see some of the sights I witnessed as a kid.

During our trip we drove up to the Grand Canyon. Fog had covered the entire viewing area. I was upset. We traveled all the way from the East Coast to see the Grand Canyon and now my wife couldn't appreciate it. As the day progressed the fog slowly lifted. I parked the car and gathered my camera gear and started taking photos. A few minutes later, Tammy walked over to the edge of the canyon and looked down into it. When I say she was on the edge I mean she was on the EDGE. I brought my new bride all the way to Arizona only for her to fall into the Grand Canyon! I was terrified. I begged her to back up. She said something like, "It's a better view from here."

How often have you been afraid to go to the edge of an opportunity, to take risks, or to realize amazing potential for your life because other people told you it wasn't safe? How often have people begged you to back up from your dreams...your goals?

Those who succeed are those who ignore the doubters around them. Horace Bushnell said, "The more difficulties one has to encounter, within and without, the more significant and the higher in inspiration his life will be."

Your persistence can make the. In *An Iron Will*, Orison Swett Marden quotes Charles Sumner as saying, "Three things are necessary: first, backbone; second, backbone; third, backbone."

You have a choice to seize your destiny or to let it pass you by. Seize it!

10

Move to a
New State!?!

"I can't move to a new state," you say? I'm not talking about a literal state (if you live in the US) but a *state of mind*. I am blown away by how much power the mind has over the way we perceive things. Have you ever had a dream or watched a movie where your body acted as if you were actually doing what you were seeing? It happens to me all the time. When I watch police chase bad guys I am in the car with them. When I see someone climbing a tall building my hands get sweaty. When I watch a sad story on television I get tears in my eyes.

How many times you found yourself in a state of mind that is not healthy for you to maintain for a long period of time? Anger, stress, fear, anxiety, and despair are examples of how our mind can cripple us from being effective. I am amazed how many people have found it possible to take life's negative situations, reframe them, and turn them into something good. Studies have concluded that people who have a purpose in life seem to be able to bounce back from unpleasant situations. I'm sure you've heard the term, "If you do what you've always done you will get what you've always gotten." Tony Robbins has a habit of saying, "Life is a gift, and it offers us the privilege, opportunity, and responsibility to give something back by becoming more." Get that? It's our responsibility to become more!

Jo Marchant, in *New Scientist*, writes, *In a study of 50 people with advanced lung cancer, those judged by their doctors to have high spiritual faith responded better to chemotherapy and survived longer. Over 40 percent were still alive after three years, compared with less than 10 percent of those judged to have little faith. There are thousands of studies purporting to show a link between some aspect of religion—such as attending church or praying—and better health. Religion has been associated with lower rates of cardiovascular disease, stroke, blood pressure and metabolic disorders, better immune functioning, improved outcomes for infections such as HIV and meningitis, and lower risk of developing cancer.*

There it is! Just one example of how changing your state can make a profound difference in your life. Tony Robbins says, "Whatever happens, take responsibility." You *must* take every difficulty, disappointment, and setback as a means to make you stronger and not to keep you down.

You have the choice to change your state of thought in order to live a life you've always imagined. Move to a different state and watch your life change for the better!

11

Reframe Your Life!

...and I'm not talking about changing the frame around a photograph or a painting. I'm talking about how you see and respond to what is going on around you. The dictionary definition of reframing is *to look at, present, or think of (beliefs, ideas, relationships, etc.) in a new or different way.* Robert L. Sandidge and Anne C. Ward describe it this way:

> *Context reframing is taking an experience that seems to be negative...and showing how the same behavior or experience can be useful in another context. For example, the other reindeer made fun of Rudolph's bright, red nose; but that funny nose made Rudolph the hero on a dark night. Content reframing is simply changing the meaning of a situation—that is, the situation or behavior stays the same, but the meaning is*

changed. For instance, a famous army general reframed a distressful situation for his troops by telling them that "We're not retreating, we're just advancing in another direction."

There is a huge advantage to reframing: it enables you to give a new meaning to a situation in your present *or* in your past. In other words, you can choose whether the glass is half full or half empty even if you drank the water 20 years ago.

Reframing can take people from despair to hope, from discouragement to optimism, from fear to courage. Years ago I avoided driving in Washington, DC. Looking at the map of the city I felt I would surely get lost. It took a friend to explain to me how simple it really was to navigate. He helped me reframe my attitude and today I have no problem driving in the nation's capital.

Every great man, every successful man, no matter what the field of endeavor, has known the magic that lies in these words: every adversity has the seed of an equivalent or greater benefit. —W. Clement Stone

How many people do you know who have made conclusions based upon information that needed to be reframed? Many people have a concept of "Learned Helplessness." W. Clement Stone would always say, "That's good!" when something challenging came along. This man chose to reframe the negative situations in his life and devise alternatives to his challenges.

Bondage is subjection to external influences and internal negative thoughts and attitudes. —

All of us have a choice to look at situations in our lives from many angles and to seek input from other people. "Wise people," wrote M. Scott Peck, "learn not to dread but actually to welcome problems." Your attitude is critical! Look at what is holding you back and write down several ways you can reframe what you can do about it.

12

What Are You Waiting For?

You've seen them…I've seen them: people with grand ideas, huge plans, and amazing talent who never seem to get off the ground. Let's be honest…you and I have been there too.

Charlie "Tremendous" Jones said, …*a sense of urgency is that feeling that lets you know yesterday is gone forever, tomorrow never comes. Today is in your hands. It lets you know that shirking today's task will add to wasted yesterdays and postponing today's work will add to tomorrow's burden. The sense of urgency causes you to accomplish what today sets before you…* Mr. Jones was right!

I have seen people with great potential live their entire lives without ever even getting started. One of the biggest obstacles they face is the fear of failure. The fear of falling on your face, of messing up and getting dirty. Someone once said, "Procrastination is opportunity's natural assassin." Michael Jordan said, "I've failed over and over and over again in my life. And that is why I succeed." He missed more shots than most other basketball players. Why? He *took* more shots…he made more attempts. That's why he is one of the greatest basketball players of all time. Steven Spielberg dropped out of high school and applied to attend film school three times but was unsuccessful due to his C-grade average. Albert Einstein learned to speak at a late age and performed poorly in school.

Elvis Presley, one of the best-selling artists of all time, is a household name even years after his death. Back in 1954, Elvis was still a nobody. Jimmy Denny, manager of the Grand Ole Opry, fired him after just one performance, telling him, "You ain't goin' nowhere, son. You ought to go back to drivin' a truck."

Think of all the massively successful people you have seen on television and movies, or heard on the radio. All of them struggled to reach their level of success. They paid the price, they cried the tears, they pushed through the discouragement and stuck with it until they achieved their dreams. This is a consistent pattern in all successful people.

Samuel Smiles said, *The battle of life is, in most cases, fought uphill; and to win it without a struggle were perhaps to win it without honor. If there were no difficulties there would be no success; if there were nothing to struggle for, there would be nothing to be achieved. He who never made a mistake, never made a discovery. The work of many of the greatest men, inspired by duty, has been done amidst suffering and trial and difficulty. They have struggled against the tide, and reached the shore exhausted.*

Over the years I have learned that those who reach massive levels of success fail often. The difference between them and those who do not succeed, however, is that they keep going and going and going. You can too! I know you've messed up, dropped the ball, and given in to discouragement. It is time to believe in yourself and the potential that resides in your being.

13

"…Pay Less Attention…"

Andrew Carnegie said, "As I grow older, I pay less attention to what men say. I just watch what they do." Mr. Carnegie lived in the early 1900's and made millions and millions of dollars in the steel industry. He was one of the first executives to recognize people who went beyond the call of duty. In today's world people say a lot of things that do not match their actions. This has been played out in the news over and over again.

There is something to be said for people who go beyond the call of duty. We witness their achievements all the time. Firemen, police officers, and military heroes come to mind, but there are others as well. Anyone who shares their time, resources, experience, strength, and courage is an example of someone who is extraordinary. A perfect example is Nelson Mandela. He said,

"What counts in life is not the mere fact that we have lived. It is what difference we have made to the lives of others that will determine the significance of the life we lead."

Every positive mark you make in the world leaves ripples in the lives of others. Those ripples create hope, encouragement, courage, and tenacity to so many people who struggle from day to day.

Be a "Doer" and not a "Sayer"!

14

Trap of
the Treadmill

In my book *Rising from the Hood: The Cure for America's Cities* there is a chapter called "The Herd" which includes this excerpt from a July 2005 article in the *Washington Post*:

It all started with one self-destructive leap. Shepherds eating breakfast outside the town of Gevas, Turkey, were surprised to see a lone sheep jump off of a nearby cliff and fall to its death. They were stunned, however, when the rest of the nearly 1,500 sheep in the herd followed, each leaping off of the same cliff. When it was all over, the local Aksam newspaper reported that "450 of the sheep perished in a billowy, white pile" (those that jumped from the middle and end of *the herd were saved as the pile became higher and the fall more cushioned). The estimated loss to the families of Gevas tops $100,000—an extremely significant amount of money in a country where the average person earns about $2,700 annually. "There's nothing we can do. They're all wasted," said Nevzat Bayhan, a member of one of the 26 families whose sheep were grazing together in the herd.*

There are hundreds of thousands of people (maybe millions) who live their lives on the "treadmill." They get on it every morning and don't get off of it until they go to sleep. They follow the same routine and do what others do because others are doing it. I will never forget the words of Charles "Tremendous" Jones, who said, "You will be the same person in five years as you are today except for the people you meet and the books you read." That quote has stuck with me for years.

Think about the sheep in the above story. Imagine, for a moment, if the great Michael Jordan did not take advice and coaching from Phil Jackson? Would he have achieved the incredible scores he was able to achieve? No one knows, but we can all assume he would have certainly done less than he achieved. Many people make a decision not to place themselves in situations where they can learn and grow, then, by default they put a glass ceiling over their future. The trap of the treadmill is designed to entice you to think that if others are doing a thing then you should too. Here are a few questions to ask yourself to see if you might be trapped by the treadmill in your life.

Does my life look the same as it did a year ago?

Have I read books about people who are doing what I imagine myself doing?

Am I doing what I am doing because of pressure from other people?

The great Coach Vince Lombardi said, "We would accomplish many more things if we did not think of them as impossible."

Break from the herd...stop the treadmill and begin to live YOUR life!!

15

Your Life Sentence

If you had the opportunity to write a *life sentence* for yourself — that is, a sentence that describes where you're going in life— what would it say? Most people never consider a *life sentence* for themselves. Someone once said that those who don't have a clear life-goal for themselves are "average and ordinary." I know that you are NOT one of them because you're reading this book with hopes of learning something new that can help you now and in the future!

John C. Maxwell said, "If you grow you will change." In an inverse statement, "If you want to change you need to grow." The truth is that most people are afraid to grow (or, worse, have no interest in growing) then complain that their life is the "same ole same ole." Here is one secret of super-successful people: they

BUILD YOUR FOUNDATION

realize that *CHANGE is KEY to their MASSIVE SUCCES*. They understand that they cannot change the past but they *can* use the past as a stepping stone and not a stumbling block. They realize that their personal attitude should mirror their potential. The truly successful realize that people behave in a manner consistent with their beliefs. William Pitt, 1st Earl of Chatham, said, "I trample upon impossibilities." Alexander the Great once said, "There is nothing impossible to him who will try." Your unwavering aim will get you to your goals but you have to identify those goals for you and for your life.

If your actions have been inconsistent with where you want to go in life, try the following:

Don't Complain...about anything.

- Stop using negative words.

- Write down one sentence that describes where you want to go in life but write it in the present tense ("I am....") and keep it in front of you ALL THE TIME!

- Understand that personal growth comes from consistent internal change.

- You have the exact same capacity as any other human being on earth regardless of your past.

- Ask daily for divine help in your endeavors.

- READ READ READ material that can help you get closer to your dreams and goals.

You can be on the edge of realizing something incredible in your life. Don't quit...don't give up!!

16

My Kids' Christmas Lists

In mid-November of each year my kids start putting together their Christmas wish lists. With six kids it gets hectic with all of them giving my wife their lists then changing the items on them all the time. Looking at the lists got me thinking. Many of us use grocery lists, birthday lists, house-hunting lists, but very few have *life lists*. Most people go through life with no idea where they will end up. They have no game plan. I'm sure you've gone to the grocery store without a list and when you got home you realized you forgot a few things. Don't live your life this way!

Our kids go through their Christmas lists then check them twice...three times...four times...you get the idea. Some may say, "I don't need to write down lists or goals that I want to achieve." Brian Tracy suggests, "Living your life without goals and objectives is setting off across unknown territory with no road signs and no road map." Without lists or goals, you will never arrive at your destination. How can you when you don't know where your destination *is?*

Know your destination! Create a *life list.* Here's what you need:

It must have DETAILS, DETAILS, DETAILS. Don't be vague about your goals and dreams. Be specific!

It has to be MEASURABLE! How will you track your progress toward your dreams and goals?

It must be REALISTIC! Keeping it real but not *too* easy will pull you toward your goals and dreams.

It must have a DEADLINE! Without a deadline you will never have the motivation to push on.

Your life list can keep you focused when life's distractions try to get you off course. You can always go back to it to remind you where you are and where you're headed. That way, when people enter your life and don't want to go in your direction you will have no problem telling them *no* to their plans for your life.

17

My Divorce!

Imagine you live in Washington, DC and you want to take a plane trip to Disney World in Orlando, Florida. You buy your ticket, drive to the airport, and run into an old friend. He convinces you to fly with him to Toronto, Canada which is in the opposite direction from Disney World. You get to Toronto and shadow your friend while he does all he wants to do. Deep down inside, however, you *really* want to go to Disney World but you don't want to offend your friend.

Fast-forward six months. You have another week of vacation and you buy another ticket to Orlando so you can finally go to Disney World. This time you run into another friend at the airport who convinces you to fly to Texas to visit some hold high school friends. Again, you succumb to the persuasion of your friend and you are miserable the entire week. You never do get to go to Disney World.

This little parable reminds me of how 97% of the public continues to chase other people's dreams instead of identifying and chasing their own. I used to be in that group. One day, after several weeks of reading great books on self-development, I decided to get a divorce! Not a divorce from my wife of now twenty-three years and about whom I am absolutely nuts, but the people who kept convincing me to realign my life's plans to *their* life's plans. Has this happened to you?

Jim Rohn said, "Run away from the 97%." Each of us has to make the decision to divorce ourselves from people who drag us down and stand in our way. I don't know about you but I'm not getting any younger, so for me, (and maybe for you) to live a life that is constantly at the beck and call of those who do not care about my goals and my dreams is unwise. True friends will help you find and follow your "Disney World Experience." These people will encourage you to step out of your box, climb every mountain, dream BIG dreams, and not be afraid!

Find the friends who will propel you forward and divorce those who continue to drag you down, hold you back, and do not believe in *your* potential!

18

So Many Distractions

The older I get the more I see the growing number of distractions that keep people from realizing their mission in life. What areas in your life seem to be crowding out the important things? From iPads to Android phones to cable television we are bombarded with ways to use our time. Denis Waitley describes these as *Tension-Relieving Activities instead of Goal-Achieving Activities.*

Christopher Columbus said, "By prevailing over all obstacles and distractions, one may unfailingly arrive at his chosen goal or destination." Imagine if Columbus would have been distracted by every storm he faced when we was looking for the Americas. He faced so many people telling him he was crazy for setting out on a journey when many thought the Earth was flat. We Americans are thankful that he persisted.

David McCullough wrote, "I'm very aware how many distractions the reader has in life today, how many good reasons there are to put the book down." Since modern technology has evolved, we see so few people who have library cards and who read books that can help them *grow* in life. My father instilled in me the value of the wealth of information in good books. My personal library consists of more than three hundred books on subjects that help me grow as an individual, a leader, and a business owner.

Larry Dixon wrote, "Winning teams have the least amount of distractions. They have a really tight group of people working towards the same common goal." Imagine if you surrounded yourself with people who believe in you, are smarter than you, earn more than you, and are more grounded in their faith than you. How different would your life be in just a few years? This can be accomplished but it's up to you to locate those individuals and "attach" yourself to them on a consistent basis. If you want to change your life in a huge way, choose to associate with the right people every day and start building and *reading* a personal library that is rich with details to help you grow!

Grenville Kleiser wrote, "The ability to apply your mind steadily and exclusively to one subject at a time is a mark of superior power and essential to really great achievement." Today, we have a world that promotes multitasking. We drive while we talk on the phone; we drive while we eat, read, and watch television; and so on. The more "stuff" we have as a society the less focused we tend to be from day to day. Louis Pasteur said, "Let me tell you the secret that has led me to my goal. My strength lies solely in my tenacity." Thomas Edison is a perfect example of a person with proactive persistence. When he reached experiment 9,999 he was asked by a reporter, "Sir, are you going to fail 10,000 times?" Edison confidently replied, "I have not failed at each attempt; rather I've succeeded at discovering another way not to invent an electric lamp."

Develop good habits and watch your life change!

19

Mental Toughness!

In order to thrive in this economy you must have *mental toughness!* In the 1939 movie *The Wizard of Oz* there's a scene where the Cowardly Lion, who is typically afraid of his own shadow, agrees to lead the assault on the castle of the Wicked Witch of the West. He dipped into his untapped stores of mental toughness and accomplished something that he never believed he could do.

Having Mental Toughness is more than just saying you have it. You have to cultivate it. First of all, be sure to get enough rest. It's been said that weariness makes cowards of us all.

Next, get comfortable with the unfamiliar. How many opportunities have we missed because we were not aware of the possibilities that would develop if we applied a small amount of effort and moved beyond our comfort zones into the realm of the unfamiliar? At 211 degrees water is hot, but at 212 degrees it boils over and makes a mess. That one degree makes all the difference in the world.

Applying one extra degree of temperature to water means the difference between something that is simply very hot and something that generates enough force to power a machine. Make it a part of your daily routine to do something totally different from what you normally do. Hang out with people who have already achieved their goals or who are dedicated to goals similar to yours. Avoid associating with people who have the same unresolved problems or who are frustrated by their lack of achievement.

Mental toughness is the ability to keep picking yourself up regardless of what life throws at you. You have it in you! You can thrive in the middle of disappointment, despair, and discouragement. Decide to become mentally tough and do what you have to do every day to maintain that toughness.

20

Smelling the Air

Our daughter, Juliana, is going through her third journey with cancer. A few months ago I asked if she had three wishes what would they be? She thought for a minute and said, "Not to have cancer, to have a billion dollars, and a puppy." My wife and I are working on her first two wishes, but we decided to go ahead and grant her her third wish…a puppy. Juliana named her Maddie.

Recently, Maddie was outside and I noticed her smelling the air. Watching Maddie got me thinking about people. In today's rapidly-changing times it is essential for people to monitor the changes around them and have the ability to shift accordingly. The social media wave has created relationships that have been leveraged for the benefit of many. Today, people seek the advice of their friends all across the globe to help them with some of life's decisions. What if the inventors, designers, and engineers of social media hadn't "smelled the air" to foresee a need and capitalize on it?

For decades people could hop in their car, turn on the radio, and pick a station that played what they wanted to listen to, but there was a limited selection. Today, Internet radio gives the average person a chance to broadcast and listen to what they want and build an audience. Remember Steve Case, the founder of America Online? Today he describes the change makers (those who smell the air) as "those who throw custom to the wind and upset the established order of a given industry." He says, "You're not trying to do something marginally, incrementally better. You're doing something that is a fundamental paradigm shift that will have exponential impact. That means it's harder to do, but ultimately, if it's successful, the impact it has is far greater."

In today's economy it is essential that all of us "smell the air" and consider the future more than the present. What are you paying attention to? Where's your "nose" as it relates to your future? Question what is and imagine what could be. Catch— no, *invent*—the next wave and leverage it!

– B L O C K –

21

O. P. O.

I have met thousands of people over the years, some of whom live in cages. Cages? They live in the cage of O.P.O. What is O.P.O? Other People's Opinions!

Other People's Opinions can lift or crush us. There are many who are bogged down by the negative opinions of people in their past. Some of them feel that they are limited by their history or by the expectations of others. Someone once said, "Never take advice from people more screwed up than you." Steve Jobs so beautifully said, "Your time is limited, so don't waste it living someone else's life. Don't be trapped by dogma—which is living with the results of other people's thinking. Don't let the noise of others' opinions drown out your own inner voice. And most important, have the courage to follow your heart and intuition."

Most people go through life like a boat without an engine or a rudder. They are battered by life and by people. The waves of discouragement, despair, manipulation, and other people's opinions blow them from one horizon to the next. The struggle, for some, is that they have not found WHY they were born. When people find out why they were born they have an "engine" and a "rudder" for their lives that enable them to direct their own future.

The people who have made their own way in life are those who are not distracted by the "status quo" or O.P.O. Imagine if Steve Jobs, Bill Gates, Thomas Edison, Christopher Columbus, and thousands of others had wasted their lives not fulfilling why they were born because of O.P.O.

Bill Cosby once said, "I don't know the key to success, but the key to failure is trying to please everybody." If you have ten friends, each one will have a different opinion. As my father told me, "Eat the meat and spit out the bones." Listen to the advice of people older and wiser than you are and spit out the advice from those who don't have a clue.

22

The Snooze Button

Most of us hit the snooze button from time to time—that little button on top of your alarm clock that gives you a few precious extra minutes between the sheets before you have to get up and face the world. Several of my children find it difficult to wake up in the morning. One night, very late, all of our smoke detectors went off at once for some strange reason. Picture this... we have a seven bedroom house with about nine smoke detectors on the top floor and every one of them was screaming. All but one of our children slept right through the commotion, still blissfully snoozing away. Other times, before I leave for the office, I walk down the hall and say, "OK, kiddy-poos, time to get up... up, up, UP!" It's my way of trying to get them up and about for school. There are a couple of our kids who have to be told several times to get up.

How many people have you met who have all the talent in the world or, at the very least, raw talent waiting to be developed yet they find it difficult to stop hitting the snooze button in their lives? Dottie Lessard said, "To truly live life we must do the things we believe we cannot." People keep hitting the snooze button in their lives because they think they cannot accomplish what they are clearly capable of, or they think they aren't smart enough, talented enough, tough enough, etc. NOT SO! Greatness is always preceded by a desire to be great…a desire to "disconnect the snooze button," leap to your feet, and run toward opportunity. Most people get discouraged between *effort* and *reward;* that is, the delay from intentional struggle toward an ideal goal and the realization of that goal. The in-between space is the hardest of all. It requires you to *stay* focused but encourages many to *lose* focus. Malcolm Gladwell writes, "Once a musician has enough ability to get into a top music school, the thing that distinguishes one performer from another is how hard he or she works. That's it. And what's more, the people at the very top don't work just harder or even much harder than everyone else. They work much, much harder." The passive people are left behind.

Maybe you know people who were raised in homes where everyone lived a snooze button-centered life. They never quite got off the ground. This does not have to be you! Research shows that it takes an average of 10,000 hours of work to be viewed as successful in any serious task. So, based on that assessment, how can people believe they can reach their goals in life by stopping and starting all the time?

One of my favorite authors, Orison Swett Marden, wrote "Success is not measured by what you accomplish, but by the opposition you have encountered, and the courage with which you have maintained the struggle against overwhelming odds."

Don't run from those odds. Embrace them, jump from your bed in the morning, take on the world, and create a life instead of allowing others to create one for you. Live a life that you want, not what gets handed to you. Consistent concentration of effort will get you closer to your dreams than most any other means. Leverage your personal power and watch your life change right before your eyes.

– B L O C K –

23

They Struggle Too!

I can remember way back, as a kid, feeling that I was the only one with fear, intimidation, self-doubt, and other "hang-ups." The older I got and the more I became a student of people I realized that most people struggle too in some form or fashion. Very few people have it "all together." Take dyslexia for example. Did you know that Pablo Picasso, Tom Cruise, Richard Branson, Leonardo da Vinci, Thomas Edison, Henry Winkler, and Jay Leno (among many others) have or have had the condition?

Some people suffer from mood disorders, people like Abraham Lincoln, Britney Spears, Richard Dreyfuss, Harrison Ford, Ben Stiller, Carrie Fisher, and so many others. Bruce Jenner, Terry Bradshaw, Jackie Stewart, John Chambers, Charles Schwab, and Dexter Scott King all suffer from ADHD. Jennifer Aniston, Cher, and Whoopi Goldberg have a fear of flying. Billy Bob Thornton is afraid of antique furniture. Johnny Depp, Daniel Radcliffe, and Sean "Diddy" Combs are frightened of clowns. Country singer Lyle Lovett is terrorized by cows. Nicole Kidman fears butterflies. Madonna is afraid of thunder. Woody Allen is afraid of insects, sunshine, dogs, deer, bright colors, children, heights, small rooms, crowds, cancer, and anywhere except Manhattan. A Harris Poll found that 86 percent of adults and 91 percent of youngsters admitted to being very afraid of something. Nearly one in five adults also said they are scared of more things now than they were as a child.

These are just a few examples of the problems faced by celebrities who many people assume have it all together. What about you? Are you going to let your insecurities, past mistakes, fears, and other "hang-ups" keep you from identifying and chasing after your dreams? Don't do it! Surround yourself with people who *believe in you* and will encourage you to stay on course regardless of what struggles you face in your life!

24

The Horn and Horn Experience

The Horn and Horn Smorgasbord was a place that my brother and I loved to go as kids. It was a restaurant that allowed patrons to (as I called it) "pick your own food." As a kid, it was the BEST place to eat. I could get as many mashed potatoes as I wanted. I didn't have to get peas or spinach (which I now love) and could get as much of anything as I liked. Oh, and the desserts...so many choices!

The Horn and Horn experience reminds me of many people in today's society. People have the opportunity, in many cases, to create their own future but insist upon having other people make those decisions for them. In Robert Kiyosaki's book, *Rich*

Dad/Poor Dad, he discusses how we think about our employment future. Kiyosaki often refers to The CASHFLOW Quadrant, a conceptual tool which he developed to categorize the four major ways income is earned. Depicted in a diagram, this concept entails four groupings, split with two crossed lines (one vertical and one horizontal). In each of the four groups there is a letter representing a way in which an individual may earn income.

E: Employee—Working for someone else.

S: Self-employed or small-business owner—A person owns his own job and is his own boss (dentist, plumber, barber, painter etc).

B: Business owner—A person who owns a business to make money; typically where the owner's physical presence is not required.

I: Investor—Investing money in order to receive a larger income in the future.

Most Americans are in the Employee Quadrant; that is, they are told when to show up, what to do, and when to go home. That is not a Horn and Horn experience. The Business Owner Quadrant is the one I would like you to consider...even if it's part time.

The Business Owner Quadrant gives you leverage in your life. One of the companies I owed had dozens of employees. Each of them was earning income for their families. I, however, was earning a little income as a result of their results. You can do this too. Once I learned this (years ago) I was never the same!

Change the rules you live by. Think HORN AND HORN EXPERIENCE and pick your own life instead of others picking it for you!

25

Paying the Price

I have heard some people say they are jealous of those who have "made it". There is a common theme among those who have made it: they decided to pay the price and a little more for their success.

There is always a price. Those who choose not to pay it often find themselves working for those who *have* paid it. What are some of the things that make up that price? First is decisiveness. So many people are indecisive about their choices. Being decisive will give you an absolute edge in life.

A daily agenda is another characteristic of those who have made it. They don't wait for events to happen. They plan for them then start moving in that direction every day. Les Brown says, "If you take responsibility for yourself you will develop a hunger to accomplish your dreams." Leadership expert John C. Maxwell says, "Every worthwhile accomplishment has a price tag attached to it. The question is always whether you are willing to pay the price to attain it—in hard work, sacrifice, patience, faith, and endurance."

The price of success is only for those who really want something out of life. Those who are jealous of those who pay the price need to rethink why they are jealous. There are people who curse their situations instead of *making* the situations they desire. Tom Peters said, "There is no such thing as an insignificant improvement." Think about the doctor who last helped you or someone you know. First, she had to endure under-graduate education, then medical school, then a residency program, then a fellowship program, then they had to get a license to practice medicine and probably took other steps before she could help you. There is always a process! Are you willing to go through a process…are you willing to pay the price to get what you desire?

Meteorologist Justin Berk recently shared his story with me. He writes, *When I was 14, I was running track and playing base-ball. I had a pain in my leg that got worse over a month, and after seeing a few doctors I was diagnosed with cancer in my left tibia. I was even threatened with possible amputation. After a search for another specialist, we found out I had a staph infection in my bone. I had a quarter-sized hole drilled out, and I was in the hospital for almost two months...then home for a few more on IV treatment. It was isolating and lonely.*

After a few years, rather than wonder if I would walk right again, I made it back to run track. One doctor still thought I had cancer even a week after my surgery and told me I would lose my leg. My parent put him in his place.

I know I was lucky to recover, but I like to think that optimism and drive had something to do with it. If that helps some kids and families pull through the toughest time, perhaps they will be running their own races one day.

Decades ago, Napoleon Hill said, "Self-discipline begins with the mastery of your thoughts. If you don't control what you think, you can't control what you do. Simply, self-discipline enables you to think first and act afterward." There is something to those words. Go get it…pay the price…don't hurt others in the process…take others with you!

26

The 180-Degree Turn

What happens when, as a child, you run and hide every time your father walks in the door because he's drunk and mean as dirt? What happens when you have to hide under the steps or in the basement coal bins because your father may kill you? What happens when you see your father break several of your mother's bones on several occasions and hold a shot gun on her for hours and hours? Things like this happened to my father, in addition to many more horrors, when he was a kid.

My father's father died of a heart attack when he was only forty years old. Shortly thereafter, my father also turned to alcohol. He spiraled out of control until one day in 1968. He was in the middle of one of his rages and had my little brother by the leg ready to bash his head into a wall. He looked into my eyes and realized what he had become…a man heading down the wrong path.

Within months of this incident my father discovered what many successful people consistently leverage to guarantee their success: he surrounded himself with a *mastermind group,* a group of people who pool their knowledge and experience for their common good.

This mastermind group found him and not the other way around. Several people saw him in trouble and formed a "huddle" around him and, in time, helped him turn his life 180 degrees. Instead of him spiraling out of control, he gained vision, goals, dreams, and purpose. It was my father, however, who had to accept the love and support of others who saw greatness in him. My father's mastermind group was able to create an image in his mind of his possibilities, a life of faith, and his limitless potential. Today, my father is known in many countries as an expert in his field.

Napoleon Hill, in his classic book *Think and Grow Rich,* wrote:

> *Economic advantages may be created by any person who surrounds himself with the advice, counsel, and personal cooperation of a group of men who are willing to lend him wholehearted aid, in a spirit of PERFECT HARMONY. This form of cooperative alliance has been the basis of nearly every great fortune.*

Choose to surround yourself with people who believe in you, support you, and hold you accountable for reaching your dreams.

27

You're the Farmer!

Have you ever thought of yourself as a farmer? You say, "I live in the city and we don't even have much grass." Maybe you think, "I wear a shirt and tie, a uniform, or a skirt for work…I'm no farmer." I think you *are* a farmer, if not literally then figuratively. Each of us can be in control of much of what we reap in our lives.

What seeds are you planting? Do you water them daily? Each of us has hidden talents—seeds—that often never become realized because we don't know how to identify them or don't know how to make them grow. The first step is to look at your life and see if you're happy with its results.

If you're not happy with your current crop look back and see what you planted and how you took care of it. If you chose to, as Denis Waitley says, engage in "stress-relieving activities instead of goal-achieving activities" then it's no wonder your crop isn't what you expected.

Farmers can't sleep late if they want a record crop. They can't skip irrigation if they want a bountiful harvest. They can't get angry because their crop didn't produce much if they chose not to plant seed. Farmers are intentional about what they want from their harvest. They work deliberately, consciously, and continuously to increase the chances of a good bounty. The farmer sees his harvest before he reaps it! He's like the ant who works all summer for the winter. Farmers are willing to rise with the sun and work until after dark every single day!

The farmer, like you and I, has to pay the price for a good crop before—*way* before—the harvest. The farmer knows that he can't expect a great harvest without a lot of time spent planting and watering. Zig Ziglar says, "The elevator to success is out of order, but the stairs are always open." A farmer knows that he can't have a harvest without a time of planting seeds.

Every successful farmer learns about the newest tools, techniques, and breakthroughs that could help his farm. This goes for us as well. Learn from the experts in areas where you want to excel. Read their books, listen to their audio programs, attend their seminars, and watch your life transform. Your commitment to self-development must be like bathing. It must be done daily or everyone around you will know it.

Brian Tracy writes in his book *No Excuses! The Power of Self Discipline,* "To become someone that you have never been before, you must first do something you have never done before." You own your own farm! You are responsible for your own harvest! Your seeds have life in them! Never underestimate your power!

28

"I Quit Quitting"

It's so easy to throw in the towel when life isn't being fair. It's so easy to run the other way when situations seem overwhelming. Sometimes life throws you a curve ball and you just don't know how to handle it. Quite a few years ago, while reading some great books, I realized something that few people understand. We often assume that the people who make it in life are super extraordinary or super smart or have super genes. *Not so!!!*

The people who make it in life develop one critical habit: they NEVER EVER QUIT!! This was eye-opening to me because I saw myself as pretty ordinary. When I started researching the lives of those who have become great at what they do I realized they just refused to quit...they refused to give up...they refused to take no for an answer. There's a Japanese Proverb that says it best: "Fall seven times, stand up eight."

QUIT QUITTING!! When you quit you have to go all the way back to the beginning of your goals and dreams in life. How about you? Are you on the edge of greatness? Are you one failure away from really making it big-time?

29

Go Ahead and Fail!

Most people are taught that failure is bad. I still remember the pain when my first-grade teacher gave me a big orange "U" (for Unsatisfactory) on one of my writing assignments. Most of us go through grade school and high school with a certain level of anxiety about failure, an anxiety that leaks into adulthood. Most people do not even like to attempt new ventures or opportunities because of that little demon on their shoulder who says, "DON'T DO IT…YOU'RE GOING TO FAIL!"

I know someone who lives in the country. Birds constantly build nests in her hanging baskets above her front porch. She brushes them out of the baskets and within a few days the birds rebuild their nests. Are birds smarter than people? Many of us give up after we get knocked down over and over...not birds! What about you? When you fail do you give up the first, second, third time? I hope not because the fourth attempt may be when you achieve your breakthrough!

Bill Gates of Microsoft was a college dropout. Thomas Edison held 1,093 patents. His teacher told him he was stupid. Basketball icon Michael Jordan was told he "didn't have enough skill." Jordan says: *"I've failed over and over again...that is why I succeeded."* Steven Spielberg was placed in a "learning disabled" class. According to Walt Disney, "You may not realize it when it happens, but a kick in the teeth may be the best thing in the world for you." Napoleon Hill, author of *Think and Grow Rich,* said, *"Opportunity often comes disguised in the form of misfortune or temporary defeat."* There are millions more people known and unknown who looked failure in the eye and kept going!

There is a profound difference between failing and quitting. Everyone fails; champions, however, never quit! They get knocked down, readjust their stance and attack strategies, and go for it as long and as many times as it takes to achieve victory! Every single day you have to decide that no matter what, you are NOT going to quit!

Sir Winston Churchill once said, "Never give in, never give in, never, never, never, never–in nothing, great or small, large or petty–never give in except to convictions of honor and good sense."

Don't be afraid of failing! Learn from each failure, readjust, and go for it again until you succeed!

30

The Kitchen Sink

Have you ever had challenge after challenge thrown at you…including the kitchen sink? I know it's happened to me! What can you do when such events hit you back-to-back? There is a story that reminds me how I should act when life's storms hit from time to time.

Years ago, a farmer owned land along the Atlantic seacoast. He constantly advertised for hired hands. Most people were reluctant to work on farms along the Atlantic. They dreaded the awful storms that raged across the sea, wreaking havoc on the buildings and crops. As the farmer interviewed applicants for the job, he received a steady stream of refusals.

Finally, a short, thin man, well past middle age, approached the farmer. "Are you a good farm hand?" the farmer asked him. "Well, I can sleep when the wind blows," answered the little man.

Although puzzled by this answer, the farmer, desperate for help, hired him. The little man worked well around the farm, busy from dawn to dusk, and the farmer felt satisfied with the man's work. Then one night the wind howled loudly in from offshore.

Jumping out of bed, the farmer grabbed a lantern and rushed next door to the hired hand's sleeping quarters. He shook the little man and yelled, "Get Up! A storm is coming! Tie things down before they blow away!"

The little man rolled over in bed and said firmly, "No sir. I told you, I can sleep when the wind blows."

Enraged by the response, the farmer was tempted to fire him on the spot. Instead, he hurried outside to prepare for the storm. To his amazement, he discovered that all of the haystacks had been covered with tarpaulins. The cows were in the barn, the chickens were in the coops, and the doors were barred. The shutters were tightly secured.

Everything was tied down.

Nothing could blow away. The farmer then understood what his hired hand meant, so he returned to his bed to also sleep while the wind blew.

That story got me thinking. As long as you and I do all we can do, then the only option we have is to rest in the fact that all we can do is all we can do. The hired hand was proactive about the storms. The farmer was reactive. What about you?

So, before life's storms start heading your way and the "kitchen sink" is being thrown at you, decide to stand and fight...and be sure you have done all you can do!

31

Weebles Wobble

In the 1970's, Playskool introduced a product called Weebles. They were egg-shaped toys that, when tilted or knocked over, would right themselves due to a small weight hidden in the bottom of each of the toys. Their slogan was *Weebles Wobble but they don't fall down.*

I've been thinking about these little toys for some time and, for me, there is a lesson in their design. President Nelson Mandela is said to have said, "The greatest glory in living lies not in never falling, but in rising every time we fall." If you are like most people it is tempting to remember the times you have failed or made mistakes. It seems that time after time those errors want to keep you from trying new things.

Some think that wobbling is a bad thing and a sign of defeat or failure. This is not true. In fact, in my experience, those who wobble the most and bounce back are the ones who really succeed. In other words, if you're not getting knocked back or knocked down too often you may not be trying to make progress. I am not a huge sports fan but when I do watch sports I notice that when players are knocked down they do not stay down. In fact, they spring to their feet to play some more.

Getting knocked down is not a sign of defeat but a sign that you are moving forward. I have met a lot of people over the years. All those who ever accomplished anything got knocked down over and over again but they always got back up and kept going. Jim Rohn said, You must constantly ask yourself these questions: *Who am I around? What are they doing to me? What have they got me reading? What have they got me saying? Where do they have me going? What do they have me thinking? And most important, what do they have me becoming? Then ask yourself the big question: Is that okay?*

Those whom we choose to hang around will have a profound effect on our abilities to keep moving forward when we wobble in our trek toward our goals. These people will either pick us up and encourage us or urge us to quit and give up.

By design, there is no way that Weebles *can't* right themselves. They were created not to stay toppled over on their side via a counter-balance to help the toy "bounce back" from being pushed over. I have some counter-balances in my life to keep me from staying toppled over when I get knocked down.

I choose to read books about people who have achieved greatness. In my office there are little reminders in pictures, paper weights, or decorations. Some of them include, *If you can dream it you can do it,* by Walt Disney; another says, *I must do the most productive thing possible at any given moment,* by Tom Hopkins; while another says, *If you don't make dust you eat dust,* by an unknown cowboy.

Like a Weeble, you have the capacity to get back up when you wobble!

32

Jenny's Pony Tail

In the early morning hours of January 3, 2013 I was in the emergency room of Sinai Hospital in Baltimore. My wife, Tammy, had spent days in bed and in pain. The medication she was on was not working, so we were at Sinai for twelve long hours trying to figure out what was wrong with her.

I was going "stir-crazy". I didn't want to fall asleep in those overnight hours because I still had to drive home. As I walked down the hall in the emergency room at about 2:20 am, while my wife rested in the ER waiting for test results, I saw a nurse trying to save the life of a twenty-four-year-old male as she did chest compressions on him. Her name was Jenny and her dark pony tail bounced up and down as she worked. She couldn't have been more than twenty-eight years old. The look in her eyes was so intense. I remember she looked right at me as I passed the room where the young man lay lifeless. She was determined to make a difference! What I did not know until after the incident was that Jenny was one of several nurses who worked tirelessly to save that young man that early morning of January 3, 2013. Despite their best efforts, he did not make it.

Life is precious. The intensity of the nursing staff gave me something to think about as I stood leaning on the door frame taking in every sound, every gesture, every smile, every moistened eye, and every movement. I saw people from every walk of life, and they choose to work together for the benefit of total strangers. This does not happen accidentally. At Sinai Hospital it is a way of life...a culture...a mission for all those who are hired by that institution.

Is life that precious to you? Do you go out of your way to make a difference in the lives of total strangers? When was the last time you engaged in a random act of kindness for someone who can never pay you back? Just think...I bet the majority of the nurses I saw that early morning never even get a thank you from the people they have helped. There must be something deeper that makes nurses do what they do. They want to make a difference!

No one is too small to make a difference. Nurse Jenny is tiny but she did all that she could! She put her heart, her body, her passion, her life into trying to save that young man. Each of the nurses who worked on him leveraged their experience, energy, and talents to try to make a difference!

With whom do you link arms every day to change the lives of others? Actress Sasha Azevedo once said, "The world is not interested in what we do for a living. What they are interested in is what we have to offer freely—hope, strength, love, and the power to make a difference!"

Begin today. Look beyond your own comfort zone, and your own family and friends, and make a difference!

33

The Scars

Some time ago I read a story that has touched many people's lives. I adapted it to make a point.

Some years ago on a hot summer day in south Florida a little boy decided to go for a swim in the old swimming hole behind his house. In a hurry to dive into the cool water, he ran out the back door, leaving behind shoes, socks, and shirt as he went. He flew into the water, not realizing that as he swam toward the middle of the lake, an alligator was swimming toward the shore. Back in the house, his mother was looking out the window and saw the two as they got closer and closer together. In utter fear, she ran toward the water, yelling to her son as loudly as she could. Hearing her voice, the little boy became alarmed and made a U-turn to swim back. It was too late. Just as he reached her, the alligator reached him.

From the dock, the mother grabbed her little boy by the arms just as the alligator snatched his legs. That began an incredible tug-of-war between the two. The alligator was much stronger than the mother, but the mother was much too passionate to let go. A farmer happened to drive by, heard her screams, raced from his truck, took aim and shot the alligator. Remarkably, after weeks and weeks in the hospital, the little boy survived. His legs were extremely scarred by the vicious attack of the animal. And on his arms were deep scratches from where his mother's fingernails dug into his flesh in her effort to hang on to the son she loved. The newspaper reporter, who interviewed the boy after the trauma, asked if he would show him his scars.

The boy lifted his pant legs. And then, with obvious pride, he said to the reporter, "But look at my arms. I have great scars on my arms, too. I have them because my mom wouldn't let go."

You and I can identify with that little boy. We have scars, too. No…not from an alligator, or anything quite so dramatic, but, the scars of a painful past. Some of those scars are unsightly and have caused us deep regret. In the midst of your struggle, there was somebody…somewhere holding on to you.

The swimming hole of life is filled with peril. That's when the tug-of-war begins, and if you have the scars of someone's love on your arms be very, very grateful.

This story touched me in a special way because so many people are ashamed of their scars, their hurts, and their mistakes. People hide them and bury them so deep that they rarely show up, or they show up as anger, pessimism, or sarcasm. What if you viewed your "life scars" as a reminder that you are a survivor... no...check that...someone who has *thrived* despite the pain of the past?

What if you looked at your past as a stepping stone to better things in your life versus a stumbling block? What if you looked at your scars and leveraged them to create an extraordinary life for yourself and for others.

You could be the means of saving someone else's life from the "alligators". Choose to change your focus to making a difference in the lives of other people who don't know how to leverage their own scars.

34

What's On
Your Hook?

Have you ever tried to communicate with someone and felt like you were talking to a brick wall? I'm sure this has happened to most of us more times than we care to remember. I have some friends who like to fish and they have told me that different types of fish are attracted to different kinds of lure or bait. That got me thinking! What if we used different "bait," in an ethical manner, when trying to influence or communicate with others? People tend to try to communicate in ways that make themselves feel comfortable. What if that is reversed? *What if we consider thinking about communicating in a manner that feels most comfortable to the one we are trying to influence?*

This can be achieved, but there are a couple of steps to accomplishing this feat. The first is **LISTENING** to not only what the other party is trying to tell you, but in what **FORM** the communication occurs. That is, what **WORDS, PHRASES,** and **HAND GESTURES** are used to try to get the point across? If you **LISTEN** carefully, and **FEED** those words and actions back to the person to whom you are communicating, the person will be more open to what you are saying. Most people don't listen when conversation is taking place, thus missing vital clues that can help the conversation. *If these skills are mastered some of the most stressful conversations can become civil.*

There's a story written thousands of years ago about a man who walked up to an individual that his culture considered an enemy. He ignored this rule and asked questions rather than TELLING what he thought was right. This act influenced dozens of people in a manner that had not been seen before up to that time. Stephen Covey says, "Seek first to understand; then be understood." As in fishing, it's important, if you want your communications to go well, to ATTRACT those you are attempting to influence with bait that lures them to an understanding of your message.

35

"I Took the Liberty…"

It was July 2007. My daughter, Juliana, who was then five years old, was struggling through cancer for the first time. My boss called one morning and said, "I took the liberty of cleaning out your office…where do you want me to put your stuff?" Instantly, my life changed! My wife and I had just built our home, our Juliana was losing weight at a tremendous rate, and now I was downsized.

What do you do when life slams you in the head? What do you do when you look around and see nothing but heartache and pain? What do you do when you put your faith and trust in people and they let you down? For me, it wasn't easy or fun. To say I didn't go through an emotional rollercoaster would be a lie. A choice stood before me: what now?

Stephen Covey used to talk about the "space": the gap between what happens to you and what you do about it. It is a decision that can make or break your future. Mr. Covey said, "In the space between stimulus (what happens) and how we respond, lies our freedom to choose. We may have limited choices but we can always choose. We can choose our thoughts, emotions, moods, our words, our actions; we can choose our values and live by principles. It is the choice of acting or being acted upon."

Again, what now? For me, it took a *long* time to get past the huge disappointment of losing my job. Even now it still hurts and makes me angry. However, today I am reaching tens of thousands of people per month in spite of being downsized.

What are you going to choose to do now despite your circumstances? Do you have an immovable faith in the infinite possibilities in your life? Faith transcends logic and emotions. There's an Arabian proverb that says "All mankind is divided into three classes: those who are immovable, those who are movable, and those who move forward." St. Augustine said, "Faith is to believe what you do not see; the reward of this faith is to see what you believe."

Your choice to see beyond the disappointments in your life can be the fuel you need to exceed your wildest expectations.

36

Scarcity Thinking

People with a scarcity mentality never seem to have enough.

A cottager and his wife had a goose that laid a golden egg every day. They supposed that the goose must contain a great lump of gold in its inside, and in order to get the gold they killed it. Having done so, they found to their surprise that the goose differed in no respect from their other geese. The foolish pair, thus hoping to become rich all at once, deprived themselves of the gain of which they were assured day by day.

Where's your focus? What do you want?

What does the word *abundance* mean? It means *more than enough*. Christmas dinner was more than enough...Thanksgiving dinner was more than enough…you have more than enough potential in you to win!

Your self-worth has so much to do with what you see as *possible* in your life. Other people's negative opinions can cause us to develop a scarcity mentality about our own potential.

The *inner scars* of your life can keep you from realizing the awesomeness of life itself! When you allow the scars from your past to run your life no wind can catch your sails. Turn your back on those mistakes and discouragements and never turn back to them. People will act and prove to the world that how they see themselves is true. If people see themselves as failures they will live as failures. If people see themselves as individuals who have limitless potential they will live accordingly.

The scarcity mentality keeps people in a box…they hoard everything. They're afraid to let go and move on!

When we see ourselves as less than…we live a life as less than.

We are not animals who live lives based on instinct. We have a choice!

The way you see yourself can have a vital impact on how you see everyone and everything around you. Don't fall victim to scarcity mentality. See the abundance that you're capable of!

37

Trust but Verify!

President Ronald Reagan had a phrase that he used when building relationships with Soviet leaders in the 1980s: "Trust but Verify." It was used as the basis of transparent relationships between the superpowers.

Trust is very delicate and once trust has been eroded or destroyed some people wonder why it seems so hard for others to trust them. Trust is like handing an infant to another human being. It needs to be done with care and compassion. Trust is the glue that keeps relationships on solid ground.

Finley Peter Dunne said "Trust everybody, but cut the cards." For years I used to trust everybody. I assumed most people were basically honest. For the most part that's true. As you know, however, there are those few who do their best to use and abuse the kindness and ignorance of others. For me, I choose not to associate with those people as they have broken that trust time and time again.

At the same time it is often difficult to know which people are the ones who will abuse your trust. Indira Gandhi said, "You can't shake hands with a clenched fist." There are times when you are faced with an opportunity to build a relationship, buy a product, make an investment, or some other act that involves trust. Do your homework! Trust but verify! Confirm before you jump into something that you might regret. Pay attention to the cues that often might be ignored as they may be signs that something is not quite right.

Trust but Verify!

38

Stay In Your Lane?

Most of us are familiar with the parable of the good Samaritan...

There was once a man traveling from Jerusalem to Jericho. On the way he was attacked by robbers. They took his clothes, beat him up, and went off leaving him half-dead. Luckily, a priest was on his way down the same road, but when he saw him he angled across to the other side. Then a Levite religious man showed up; he also avoided the injured man.

A Samaritan traveling the road came on him. When he saw the man's condition, his heart went out to him. He gave him first aid, disinfecting and bandaging his wounds. Then he lifted him onto his donkey, led him to an inn, and made him comfortable. In the morning he took out two silver coins and gave them to the innkeeper, saying, 'Take good care of him.

If it costs any more, put it on my bill—I'll pay you on my way back.'

It is interesting that those who you would think would help the man did not. It took a stranger; in fact, a man from a part of the world that was hostile to the people of the man who was attacked.

We are taught to "mind our own business." When we are taught how to drive a car we are taught to "stay in your own lane." Many people choose to stay in their lane because people have "honked their horn" at them in the past when they dared change lanes.

Robert Allen said, "Everything you want is just outside your comfort zone." What if the Samaritan hadn't decided to make a difference in the life of the man who was attacked by thieves?

Look at all the people around you and have the courage to make the first move in order to impact their lives in a big way. They will be forever grateful!

– B L O C K –

39

Liquid Nitrogen
in My Arm!

In the late summer of 2011 I noticed some red blotches on my neck. I didn't worry about it much until other people started to mention it. Finally, that October, I decided to see a doctor. He told me that the blotches were because of the sun…I still don't understand it but he said it's nothing to worry about so I didn't worry about it. Since I was there anyhow, I figured I'd tell him about a freckle on my forearm that's about 6 millimeters in diameter. It's annoying and distracting. He asked me if I wanted to get rid of it. I said, "Sure."

I had noticed a container labeled *Liquid Nitrogen* on the counter of the examining room but paid it no mind until the doctor reached behind and picked it up along with a transparent funnel that was about the size of half an egg. He placed the funnel on my freckle, raised the liquid nitrogen container to its lip, and squeezed the trigger. He was pumping liquid nitrogen into my arm! My first reaction was to run (or smack him)...to get away from the pain and burning of the extreme cold. But I did not run. It seemed like the doctor pumped in the chemical forever but, in reality, it was about a minute.

What's the lesson here? Sometimes our initial response to run from pain may not be the best option. My large freckle is gone, but what if I had grabbed the doctor's arm and slapped him because he was hurting me? I'd still have the freckle.

Pain, if understood correctly (as shared by Brian Dodd), can:

- Produce strength in us.

- Provide leverage for us to learn, grow, and improve.

- Build stamina.

- Remind us to change bad behaviors.

- Bring clarity.

- Increase our capacity and patience.

For me, the short-term pain brought long-term gain. No more huge freckle.

Short-term pain is a fact of life and learning to endure it is often the key to long-term success. Harland Sanders of Kentucky Fried Chicken fame had his recipe rejected 1,009 times before a restaurant accepted it. One of Walt Disney's first bosses told him that he "lacked imagination and had no good ideas." Albert Einstein didn't speak until he was four and didn't read until he was seven. When Thomas Edison was young his teachers told his parents that he was "too stupid to learn anything." Oprah Winfrey was fired as a television reporter because, in her boss' eyes, she was "unfit for TV."

How about you? What are you going to do with your pain? Push past it or run from it?

40

Leverage Your Past

I meet people all the time with different strengths, weaknesses, and stories. There are a few who have chosen to use their past as a source of inspiration, strength, and hope for the future. Others, however, choose to use their past in a manner that keeps them from reaching up for new and better things. Can there be any lessons from a divorce, major illness, loss of a job, abuse, or manipulation? Of course!

Most of those who reach their dreams have a habit of using *all* of the information in their past and learning from it instead of stumbling over it. This takes real courage. Consider the following:

Orison Swett Marden, in *Pushing to the Front,* writes, "A spark falling upon some combustibles led to the invention of gunpowder. A few bits of seaweed and driftwood, floating on the waves, enabled Columbus to stay a mutiny of his sailors which threatened to prevent the discovery of a new world." What if there had been no spark? What if there had been no threatened mutiny? Would they have even noticed the seaweed?

Marden continues, "It was a little thing for the janitor to leave a lamp swinging in the cathedral at Pisa, but in that steady swaying motion the boy Galileo saw the pendulum, and conceived the idea of thus measuring time. The web of a spider suggested to Captain Brown the idea of a suspension bridge." What if those people would not have noticed (leveraged) the information all around them for their benefit and, eventually, the benefit of millions of people? What small events in your past could do the same?

Marden also said, "Small things become great when a great soul sees them. A single noble or heroic act of one man has sometimes elevated a nation."

Revisit your past...but briefly. Don't do it as a participant (which evokes emotions) but rather as a student (which gives knowledge). This process can help stop the habit of repeating the same mistakes over and over again without the benefit of changing your life.

Do not allow the challenges of the past to keep you from reaching forward to your dreams. Step up on those experiences, notice the lessons in each situation, pay attention to the smallest of details, and walk away with your head held high with ideas and a greater vision for your potential. As a friend told me recently, "there are many minutes in life and then there are fewer special moments." Maximize each moment (in the past and present) as leverage to propel you to your dreams and goals.

41

The Baton

Have you ever looked at other people and wondered how they are making it? I have had clients who were going through the worst situations imaginable and yet they had tranquility within them.

There comes a time when you have to decide what is going to impact your attitude. In the Olympics, the relay race uses a baton that is handed from one runner to the next. The baton is twelve inches long, smoothly cylindrical, and known as *the Stick*. In a *New York Times* story, one relay runner compared the baton exchange "...to two ships passing in the night (but if the ocean were the size of a phone booth), while another likened it to a hurried traveler's trying to catch up to (and hold hands with) his wife as he maneuvered on a moving walkway in a crowded airport. Neither one was joking."

Where am I going? Each of us carries feelings, lessons learned, and relationships that help or hinder us on our journey. The clients mentioned above decided to build a foundation of tenacity in their lives. They chose to learn lessons from people who have endured hardships and thrived. In other words, instead of becoming survivors they became people who thrive in the midst of struggle.

My youngest daughter, Juliana, has been struggling with cancer since 2007. Her mom and I handed her a "baton" of courage...of no whining...of being thankful...of one-day-at-a-time thinking....of unconditional love. She carries this "baton" wherever she goes. Whose "baton" do you carry from day to day? Is it from people who never achieved anything in their lives, people who always put you down, and people who are average and ordinary? Or is it from people who can lift you up and take you to a new level of success?

42

Maintaining Your Momentum

You're on a roll for weeks, months, maybe even years and then it all falls apart. I am sure you know someone who has gone through such a situation. If you're anything like me, the first tendency is to hit the brakes in frustration and stop moving forward. Have you ever watched NASCAR? When one car spins out the others go around it and keep moving forward. They don't allow distractions to stop them. I've seen cars lose a tire and hobble into the pit. They get fixed up and re-enter the race. They don't quit or give up!

This is a little like life. You are surrounded by people "spinning out" and, from time to time, *you* spin out. What happens afterward is critical to getting back on track. One very important asset you must have is a top notch "pit crew." That is, people in your life who can get you back in the race of life. A poor pit crew means you have little chance of winning. How do you find a good pit crew? It's easier than you think. Read about and become friends with people who have achieved a level of success that you admire. Recently, a young man contacted me from a referral I gave about a company I did business with in India. He came to my office and asked me to make him accountable. In essence, he asked me to be part of his pit crew.

Distraction and discouragement are huge hindrances to momentum. They must be overcome! For me, I surround myself with quotes, posters, books, and audio material that remind me to stay focused. Get rid of the unnecessary baggage in your life. Commit to staying focused on your goals and don't allow people or circumstances to stop your momentum.

One great way to maintain momentum is to surround yourself with people who cheer you on. This must be intentional because there are many who will put negative thoughts in your mind, create self-doubt, and share every reason in the world why you can't achieve your goals. Finally, don't whine or complain. When you do you become distracted by the past and lose faith in your ability to overcome the struggles of the present. Don't stop moving forward—your daily momentum is essential to your success!

43

Old News

There was a man who lived a long time ago by the name of Paul. He was smart and a leader in his community. Paul, however, had a mean streak. In fact, Paul was so mean that he went about having people murdered. This went on for quite some time until one day he experienced a life-changing event that dramatically repurposed his whole life.

Several times he said, "I forget about the things of the past and press forward…" Paul, the man who coordinated attacks and murders on innocent people, realized his mistakes and made the decision to leave them in the past. It blows me away.

I've met countless people who continue to carry around baggage from their past. There are people who are still grieving over a divorce that happened years ago or a relationship that was severed.

Others recall stupid things they have done when they were young and live in the "rut of regret." There are too many people who use their mistakes as a way to keep them from growing past them.

Mistakes, even the most serious ones, can keep you from getting your life out of neutral and moving forward. Regret is what keeps us from climbing the mountains in our lives. You attempt to do great things and you fail. You try again and you make mistake after mistake. The temptation is to give up and coast through life. Don't let this happen to you!

Coasting is always downhill. I have yet to see anything coast uphill. This is also true for your life. Once you identify where you are going you must decide that it is always going to be uphill. There will be a bunch of times when the mistakes of the past are going to jump in your face and scream at you to stop trying. The voices will say, "You're not good enough," "you've tried this before and you failed," and "everyone told you to be satisfied with the way things are now." You must reject the idea of looking back because your past has no place in your future.

Your past can be a way for you to stumble through life or it can be a stepping-stone to your path to victory. James Buckham writes, *Trials, temptations, disappointments—all these are helps instead of hindrances, if one uses them rightly. They not only test the fiber of character but strengthen it…Every trial endured and weathered in the right spirit makes a soul nobler and stronger than it was before.*

Every single day you have a space of time to make a decision. You can decide to allow the past to cloud your view of the amazing potential that lives inside you or you can allow the past to be an excuse for not living an outstanding life. Every single human being makes plenty of mistakes…so what? Let the past stay in the past!

44

Whom Are You Leveraging?

How often have you thought that some people who have reached massive levels of success must be either *really* smart or *really* lucky? During my teens and early twenties I thought the same thing. At some point I realized that these people, whom I see on television or in business, could not have been born that smart. I started to dig. I found out that all of these people used *leverage* to achieve their success. Leverage is defined as "the mechanical advantage gained by employing a lever." So, what's a lever? A lever is "A simple machine consisting of a rigid bar pivoted on a fixed point and used to transmit force, as in raising or moving a weight at one end by pushing down on the other."

What does this have to do with successful people? Successful people use the knowledge of *other people* to lift themselves up to higher levels of knowledge, experience, and income. Think of all the successful people you know…they all have mentors and teachers that they used to leverage themselves to reach specific goals *faster than the rest*. Virgin Records/Airlines CEO Richard Branson leveraged the knowledge and experience of Freddie Laker. Famous Film Directors Ron Howard, Martin Scorsese, James Cameron, and others all leveraged Roger Corman and now, of course, others are leveraging Ron Howard, Martin Scorsese, and James Cameron.

The key, in order to shorten your path to your dreams and goals, is to find others who have paid the price to get where you're trying to go and *get into their heads*. This must be done intentionally and consistently. Those who have gone before you have already paid the price and can save you hundreds of hours of painful mistakes that you do not have to make in *your* path to greatness.

I chose to read the books, attend the seminars, and listen to those whom I wish to emulate. Invest in yourself and your investment will carry you to your dreams—and beyond!

45

The A.S.K. Method

It was not an easy climb to the top for Sylvester Stallone. In his early days as an aspiring actor, he was broke but would not take an average job as it would interfere with his hunger to be an actor. His wife pressured him to get a job but Stallone would not hear of it. He kept trying to audition for parts but kept being rejected.

By that time he was so poor that he decided to sell his dog. He was devastated but he felt he had no choice. After desperately looking for strangers to buy his dog, he finally found a buyer outside a liquor store and sold it for $25.

After seeing Muhammad Ali at a boxing match Stallone got the idea for *Rocky* and invested twenty non-stop hours writing the screenplay. He kept trying to sell the script but kept getting rejected. Finally, someone was interested in buying but only if Stallone did not star in it! Even though he was broke, he knew what he wanted and did not sell out. They had offered to buy the script for $100,000 and they kept upping the offer until they got to $400,000 but Stallone would hear none of it unless he was the star.

Eventually they agreed to let him play the title role, but only for $25,000. He accepted and as soon as he got his money, he went to buy back his dog. The new owner refused to sell it to him! Again Stallone persisted until the guy sold it back to him for $15,000 and the right to appear in the movie!

The film, made for only $1.1 million and shot in a relatively fast 28 days, was a sleeper hit; it made over $117.2 million, and won three Oscars, including Best Picture. The film received many positive reviews, turned Stallone into a major star, and spawned five sequels.

Now, here's the "A.S.K" method:

The Bible says, *Keep on asking, and you will receive what you ask for. Keep on seeking, and you will find. Keep on knocking, and the door will be opened to you. For everyone who asks, receives. Everyone who seeks finds. And to everyone who knocks, the door will be opened.*

A– Ask and ask A LOT!

S– Seek after what you desire and work to acquire it.

K– Knock on all the doors you can until you get what you desire.

A couple thousand years ago a widow kept after a local judge: 'My rights are being violated. Protect me!'

He never gave her the time of day. But after this went on and on he said to himself, 'I care nothing what God thinks, even less what people think. But because this widow won't quit badgering me, I'd better do something and see that she gets justice—otherwise I'm going to end up beaten black-and-blue by her pounding.'

Persistence PAYS OFF!

Richard M. Devos said, "If I had to select one quality, one personal characteristic that I regard as being most highly correlated with success, whatever the field, I would pick the trait of persistence. Determination. The will to endure to the end, to get knocked down seventy times and get up off the floor saying, 'Here comes number seventy-one!'"

Aristotle asked a young man to follow him to the sea, then he asked him to jump into the sea with him. As Aristotle was a strong man, he got hold of the boy's head, submerged it under water by force, and kept him there for three minutes. When the boy started to lose in the struggle to surface and neared total drowning, Aristotle released him.

The boy was in utter shock and horror and angrily demanded from Aristotle the reason he had done that to him. Aristotle asked, "How badly did you want to breathe air, young man?" The young man answered, "Very, very badly Master, I couldn't think of anything else in the world but to breathe air". Aristotle continued, "When you desire and commit to your mission with this kind of intensity, then you have a mission on the way to becoming reality."

Pain is temporary. If you quit...pain will last forever! At the end of pain is success...at the end, pain is the open door you've been looking for.

Keep ASKING, SEEKING, and KNOCKING...ALL THE TIME!

46

Expect Backups

Traffic jams are a fact of life. When I was in my twenties I never planned for traffic jams and I was always in a hurry. I used to take out my frustrations on my steering wheel and I cracked it many times…it's pretty embarrassing sharing this with you.

People on the highway slow way down when they see an accident or someone getting a speeding ticket. It used to drive me CRAZY. Now I am a little older and (hopefully) a little wiser and I understand that life has a way of placing us in backups; that is, we are going merrily along when disaster strikes and we have to stop in our tracks. It could be illness, job loss, family issues, emotional pain, or some other struggle that forces us to stop. Then we look around and see many more people who are also stopped in their lives.

Some just sit there while others look for a detour. When we *plan* for backups or traffic jams it is so much easier to stay on track. I have four ways I can get to my office if one or more roads are backed up or blocked. In its simplest form this is called having Plan B, Plan C, and maybe Plan D...just in case.

We have a choice! We have to make the decision to reprogram our "Mental GPS" by hitting the "reroute or detour" button. The backup still exists but you *decided to find another way to get where you're going!* There's an old story of a man named Joe who was imprisoned despite his innocence. He spent years incarcerated but he stayed positive and *mentally detoured* his brain from despair to hope. When he got out he was able to get an executive position in a large family business. Sometimes, when we are faced with detours, there is an ultimate purpose for the backup.

Maybe you were headed down a road that was not going to benefit you in the long run so life sent you a backup. If you choose to take the detour it could lead you down roads that you would not otherwise have traveled. Sometimes this opens opportunities, insights, and relationships that you could never have imagined.

47

The Courage
of a U-Turn!

One of the biggest road blocks to personal progress is refusing to admit when you are wrong. How many men, while driving their car, refuse to ask for directions and refuse to turn around and go the other way because of their ego? Recently I had the opportunity to see a U-Turn in progress. I know of a young lady who has been the victim of physical abuse at the hands of her spouse. Recently, she had the courage to make a U-Turn by separating from her abusive husband. This was a huge step in the right direction!

How often do people go day after day, week after week, and month after month, heading down a wrong (or even a dangerous) road yet make the decision to keep going?

Many people get stuck in a rut. John Addison suggests that you "don't crawl out of the mud (rut) you have to explode out of the mud (rut)." Dave Anderson put it another way: "You might be in a rut if you can't remember the last time you tried something for the first time; you might be in a rut if you compare yourself to others more than to your former self; you might be in a rut if you've become comfortable living a life filled with goals mostly unrealized; and you might be in a rut if you haven't made a big mistake lately." It's not always about trying to fix something that's broken. Maybe it's about starting over and creating something better.

Eric Roth, in his screenplay for *The Curious Case of Benjamin Button*, wrote, *For what it's worth: it's never too late or, in my case, too early to be whoever you want to be. There's no time limit, stop whenever you want. You can change or stay the same; there are no rules to this thing. We can make the best or the worst of it. I hope you make the best of it. And I hope you see things that startle you. I hope you feel things you never felt before. I hope you meet people with a different point of view. I hope you live a life you're proud of. If you find that you're not, I hope you have the courage to start all over again.*

A common thread about all the people who have made it in life is the fact that they are not afraid of admitting a mistake, turning around, and making some changes in their lives. The young lady I mentioned above realized "enough is enough" and made a U-turn. So can you. Look down the road you're taking and analyze where you are headed. Don't be afraid to turn around. You have it in you!

Admitting you're wrong is not a sign of weakness; rather, it shows strength.

48

Then What Will Happen?

Stephen Covey once said, ...*between stimulus and response there is a space. Ultimately, this power to choose is what defines us as human beings. We may have limited choices but we can always choose. We can choose our thoughts, emotions, moods, our words, our actions; we can choose our values and live by principles. It is the choice of acting or being acted upon.*

In that space is the power to choose. The older I get the wider the space is between stimulus and response. What happens between the time you learn of an event and the time you act upon it?

Think about the times you have been faced with a challenge. Have you been tempted to run from it or have you had the urge to push through it? It reminds me of the fight-or-flight response that your body goes through when threatened. Dr. Neil Nei-mark describes it this way:

> When our fight-or-flight response is activated, sequences of nerve cell firing occur. These patterns of nerve cell firing and chemical release cause our body to undergo a series of very dramatic changes. Our respiratory rate increases. Blood is shunted away from our digestive tract and directed into our muscles and limbs, which require extra energy and fuel for running and fighting. Our pupils dilate. Our awareness intensifies. Our vision sharpens. Our impulses quicken. Our perception of pain diminishes. Our immune system mobilizes with increased activation. We become prepared—physically and psychologically—for fight-or-flight. We scan and search our environment, "looking for the enemy."

What if you looked for the positive possibilities instead of the negative ones when you are faced with a sudden challenge? So many people shrink back in fear and intimidation when, maybe, they should embrace the challenges that come their way. If we choose to embrace sudden opportunities we may find sides of ourselves that have been dormant for many years. Whatever comes your way can be handled, can be overcome! Muhammad Ali said, "It isn't the mountains ahead to climb that wear you out, it's the pebble in your shoe." It's the little things that can drive you crazy.

What will happen if you decide to embrace challenges as opportunities instead of threats? The Wright Brothers made four flights one day in 1903. The airplane tumbled and collapsed and was destroyed. Did it stop them? NO! They rebuilt the plane and made history! You get one life...that's it.....embrace it. Why not go for it and see what happens?

49

What Was Impossible...Isn't!

I often watch old movies and read antique books. It's amazing how far the world has come in the last hundred years. People who lived in the early 1900's could not have imagined how much technology, innovation, medicine, and knowledge would increase over time. Lately, my image of impossibility has been stretched again. Is impossible *really* impossible? What are you able to do today that you did not think was possible years ago?

What could you do tomorrow that you have not considered today? I could list hundreds of examples of people who stretched themselves in order to realize the extraordinary. Look at that word...*extraordinary*. You have extraordinary in you! People who achieve the extraordinary always, ALWAYS stretch themselves! So, how do you stretch yourself?

This is what I do in order to put myself in a *possibilty* mode versus an *average and ordinary* mindset that is happy with the way things are going right now. I subscribe to magazines and e-zines like *Success, INC, Fast Company, The Robb Report,* Jim-Rohn.com, MichaelHyatt.com, SethGodin.com and several others in order to create new connections in my brain which enable me to see past my current horizon; that is, to see past the supposed impossibilities in my life and see what others ARE doing. After all, if they can achieve what was once not in existence than so can I…and so can you!

There is one constant in all of the people I know and read about who have pushed past the impossible in their own lives: they do not base their lives on *what is;* they build their lives on *what could be!*

50

Our Greatest Weakness

These are the words of Thomas A. Edison: "Our greatest weakness lies in giving up. The most certain way to succeed is always to try just one more time." There is something to be said for someone who says not to quit and, like Mr. Edison, has "been there and done that." Mr. Edison invented or significantly improved, among other things, the incandescent light bulb, the phonograph, the movie camera, electricity distribution, the quadruplex telegraph, the stencil duplicator, and the carbon microphone.

When you think of someone like Mr. Edison you might think that all he touched turned to gold. This was not so. In fact, he failed over and over again but refused to quit! One of his failures was to use cement as an all-around building material. It never caught on.

There seems to be a common thread with those who achieve great things. When they get knocked down they refuse to stay down.

Derek Clark said, "When life knocks you down, you can either be a trier or a crier. The way you respond to challenges determines the level of success you have in life. Our yesterdays do not have to define who we are today."

In Jack Canfield and Mark Victor Hansen's *A Cup of Chicken Soup for the Soul* they write, "Colonel Sanders had the construction of a new road put him out of business in 1967. He went to over 1,000 places trying to sell his chicken recipe before he found a buyer interested in his 11 herbs and spices. Seven years later, at the age of 75, Colonel Sanders sold his fried-chicken company for a finger-lickin' $15 million!"

Albert Einstein did not speak until he was four years old and didn't read until he was seven. His teacher described him as "mentally slow, unsociable, and adrift forever in his foolish dreams." He was expelled and refused admittance to Zurich Polytechnic School. The University of Bern turned down his Ph.D. dissertation as being irrelevant and fanciful.

Margaret Mitchell's classic *Gone with the Wind* was turned down by more than twenty-five publishers.

Captain J. David Atwater, CHC, USN once said, *We all face difficulty and discouragement from time to time. We also have a choice in how we handle it. If we're persistent, if we hold fast to our faith, if we continue to develop the unique talents God has given us, who knows what can happen? We may end up with an insight and an ability to inspire that comes only through hardship.*

– B L O C K –

51

When You're Tempted to Whine

Mark Sanborn says, "Next time you start to ask 'What's wrong?', change the pattern by beginning with 'What's Right?'" I know in my life there have been times when I see only what's NOT going the way I want it to go. I look at my vision board and my written goals and see that many of them haven't come to pass...yet.

It's always eye-opening when I see how other, less-fortunate people live. I remember when we traveled to Belarus and learned that most people there live on less than thirty dollars a month. It's obvious that most of them would trade places with me any day. How about the people in Syria? They are being murdered by their own government. They would also trade places with me any day. How about the person whose child passed away? Surely, *they* would trade places with me!

How about you? It is so tempting to look at what others have and you do not. Sometimes it's frustrating. Most of the time we don't know what they've gone through to get what they have! Have you and I paid the price that they paid? Maybe…maybe not! When I lived in an apartment I wanted to live in a townhouse. When I lived in a townhouse I wanted to live in a single-family home.

When you're tempted to whine consider counting all the good things that are in your life. There's an old hymn that says, "count your blessings…name them one by one." Write down a list of all the GOOD things and people in your life…express appreciation. An attitude of gratitude will silence the temptation to whine.

Thornton Wilder wrote, "We can only be said to be alive in those moments when our hearts are conscious of our treasures." When you start to list all the good things in your life you will soon see that you are more fortunate than ninety percent of the people in the world!

52

The Steel Beam

What if I had a steel beam that was twelve inches wide and twenty feet long and I put that beam on a stage about one foot off the ground? Then, what if I asked you to walk across that beam for a prize of $50,000? Would it be very difficult? Probably not. But what if I took a beam that was twelve inches wide and two hundred feet long, suspended it hundreds of feet in the air between two skyscrapers, and asked you to walk across it for the same reward of $50,000? Oh, it also happens to be a windy day. Would you do it? Now, take the same beam and the same buildings. The building on the other side of the beam is on fire. The person you love most is inside screaming for help. The only hope for rescue is to cross the beam. Would you hesitate? Does the $50,000 really matter now?

The point here is that sometimes people don't attempt great things because their *why* isn't BIG enough. Their reason to be extraordinary isn't big enough yet! Identify your *why!* Knowing your *why* gives you great power—the power of *WHY!* When your *why* is huge you will do extraordinary things. When your *why* equals the size of our opportunity you will find out *HOW* to accomplish it...whatever it is!

Soccer star David Beckham was told, "You'll never play for England because you're too small and not strong enough." He rededicated himself and said, "I'm going to prove that coach wrong." His *why* was huge! He wanted to prove the coach wrong! When you have a vision...a reason why...you won't zig-zag on life's path. When we don't have a strong enough *why* we will never realize our *what* and our *how*. Your *WHY* pulls you toward your *WHAT* and your *HOW!*

53

The Time Machine

Let's say that tonight you go to bed and wake up the next morning to find out it's December 31st. Somehow, some way, you have been transported to the last day of the year. There are two things that will have happened. The first is that December 31st looks pretty much exactly the same as *last* New Year's Eve, OR you decided to do something *different* during the course of the year that's about to draw to a close.

Many of us allow circumstances and situations to dictate where we end up in life. There are others, however, who decide where they wish to be at a specific date in the future.

I often travel on airplanes, but only recently did I learn that planes are off course most of the time because of wind, storms, or other weather issues. The secret to the plane arriving at its destination is that the pilot makes minor course corrections during the flight to keep it heading in the right direction. First, however, there has to be a destination programmed into the flight computer. This is what each of us needs to do in order to make sure we arrive at our chosen destinations. If we don't have a destination in mind, how will we know when we arrive? How will we know when we are veering off course? Here are some ways to plan your life-course in measurable ways:

1. Write down your top five goals for the year. Write them in the present tense and be specific ("By June 2014 I lost 15 pounds by working out three days a week for at least 45 minutes a day and I will not eat anything after 9pm"). Your goals need to be "S.M.A.R.T."; That is, **S**pecific, **M**easureable, **A**ttainable, **R**ealistic and **T**imely.

2. Place those goals on your refrigerator and your bathroom mirror. This is essential to help you stay on track.

3. Make a written to-do list for the following day before going to bed each night and carry that list with you, being sure to cross off the things as you accomplish them. This may sound ridiculous, but you will be amazed by how it will help you develop "laser focus" in your life.

4. Prioritize your life in such a way that your goals become your daily priority. There will be times when you will have to say *no* to tension-relieving activities and stick to goal-achieving activities.

Brian Tracy said, "Imagine arriving on the outskirts of a large city and being told to drive to a particular home or office there. But there are no road signs and you have no map. In fact, all you have is a very general description of the home or office, so finding it would be, very much, a matter of luck. Sadly, this is the way most people live their lives."

Don't live a life of passive aimlessness. Select a destination, chart your route, and make the necessary course corrections to get you there!

54

Isolation Disease

I've had the opportunity to meet with and help thousands of people, and one thing has become clear: there is an epidemic of isolation. Sometimes a habit or a feeling of isolation comes upon people when they have been hurt and they do not want to be hurt again. Others are simply "hard-wired" to choose a life of isolation.

In *The Dangers of Loneliness*, published in the July 2003 issue of *Psychology Today*, Hara Estroff Marano says, *Friendship is a lot like food. We need it to survive. What is more, we seem to have a basic drive for it. Psychologists find that human beings have fundamental need for inclusion in group life and for close relationships. We are truly social animals.*

In my world, I learned early on that I did not have all the answers to life's problems. Back in 1983 I was working at a photo-processing lab in Baltimore. My job was sitting in a small room in total darkness and processing photographs. I fell into a deep depression and found myself crying a lot. In 1988 I found myself stuck in a dead-end job, afraid to make a change. One day I told myself that if I did not change, my life would not change. In 1988, I made a career move that transformed my life. I chose to pull myself out of my comfort zone into a life that kept me from slipping back into isolation.

If you find yourself being lonely, it's up to you to pull yourself from the comfortable, from the isolation, and create the life that you have always imagined. I found that most people are at least a little intimidated when it comes to getting out of their "box." It can be a little scary. Here's how I did it: I focused on the other person's needs, and then my own needs and fears did not seem so extraordinary.

I remember the words of Zig Ziglar: "You can have everything in life you want if you help enough people get what they want." This was the catalyst that helped me "get it." I grew up with a speech impediment and was terribly ashamed and embarrassed. Mr. Ziglar's words helped pull me from self-focus to other-people-focus and thus pulled me from my self-imposed prison of isolation.

In March 2013 about twelve members of Church 3.0 in Westminster, Maryland, led by Pastor Jeff Simmons, arranged to stop by my home and pray for our family as our daughter, Juliana, was going through her third bout with cancer. The wonderful people who came to our home pulled us from feelings of frustration and fear and lifted us up in a way that I cannot express.

There are people waiting for you to have that kind of love in your heart to pull them from despair and frustration.

If you feel isolated and alone...you're not. There are so many people just like you. There is nobody with exactly the same strengths as you. There is nobody who has the exact same dreams and goals as you. You are somebody! You are unique! Don't be ashamed of that uniqueness!

You have the capacity to make a huge difference in your life and the lives of so many people around you!

55

The Greatest Gift!

I look back on my life and consider the greatest gifts I have ever received. A few of them were things that can be held or touched with my hands. Most of them were interactions, relationships, and conversations. Society has a way of telling people that if you buy this or that you will be happy; if you eat this food or drive that car you will be happy and find fulfillment.

May I offer an alternative? The greatest gift you can give to other people is you! A you that is more focused on the needs of other people than your own; a you that gives with no expectation of something in return; a you that looks out for other people before you look out for yourself. You can be a gift that people will remember for a lifetime.

When I was a kid our family traveled throughout the Southwestern part of the United States for my father's business. My father is known as an expert in a specific era of history and during much of my childhood he was acquiring material for that business. In Bisbee, Arizona we met a man in his eighties named Robert "Shorty" O'Neal." On many occasions, Mr. O'Neal had the opportunity to make decisions that where unethical (and profitable for my father) knowing he would not have been caught. He chose, along with my father, to do business in an ethical and honorable manner. As a boy of twelve or thirteen it impacted me greatly and still drives my life today. It was a gift that has lasted for decades.

In my early twenties, I worked for a man named John Meginnis. I was painfully shy and very unsure of myself. Over time Mr. Meginnis inspired courage in me and a desire to overcome my shyness. His encouragement lives with me today. He was his gift.

There's an old saying that goes "Give, and you will receive. Your gift will return to you in full-pressed down, shaken together to make room for more, running over, and poured into your lap. The amount you give will determine the amount you get back."

When you give of yourself, with no deceit or manipulation, you will be the recipient of more than you can imagine. This has been so true for me and it will also be true for you.

Albert Einstein said, "Only a life lived for others is worth living. Our task must be to free ourselves from this prison by widening our circles of compassion to embrace all living creatures and the whole of nature in its beauty."

Take the greatest gifts that you have inside of you and create memories that will last a lifetime.

56

Thriving in Uncertainty!

Many people want to be certain about life and what is going on around them. Those who want that certainty will, more times than not, find a comfortable life. There are others, however, who do *not* like certainty. They *thrive* on the edge of knowing and not knowing what tomorrow may bring down their path. A life of certainty is predictable, calculated, and expected. A life of uncertainty is unpredictable, uncalculated, and unexpected.

There are those who choose to thrive in uncertainty. They see, taste, and feel what others cannot imagine. They see the potential while others only see what already exists. These are the same people who go hiking through Europe, or buy a franchise or, at middle age, decide to chase a life-long dream. Those who thrive in uncertainty cast aside the stereotypes they have of certain people and choose to build bridges. Thriving in uncertainty is a decision. It is a decision to be, often times, scared out of your mind! These people love being over their heads. Tyler Tervooren asks, "If I died tomorrow, would I be satisfied with how I lived my life?" Many people have died without ever really living.

So, how can you thrive in uncertainty? Tyler Tervooren gives several ways to do exactly that:

1. Call a stranger from a phone book (NOT a crank call).

2. State your unfiltered opinion (forget about "political correctness")

3. Speak up when something is wrong.

4. Try to speak a foreign language (with the help of a translation dictionary) to a native speaker.

5. Give an impromptu speech.

6. Try something you've never done before.

7. Publicly state your biggest goal.

When you purposely take on activities like the ones mentioned above, you stretch yourself to a point of thriving in uncertainty!

57

Deferred
Maintenance

Have you heard of planes crashing or parts falling off of trucks because of improper maintenance? Have you heard of people having heart attacks because they ignored the warning signs? How about people who don't change the oil in their car? How about a $50 leaking toilet valve? If not dealt with, the toilet overflows and costs thousands of dollars in damage. Deferred maintenance is the practice of *postponing maintenance activities.*

When people adopt the habit of deferred maintenance there can be long-term consequences. One of the most common problems is that people stop growing and learning when they are "done" with school. Most of my biggest challenges have been overcome, partially due to the fact that constant learning has become a habit.

Brian Tracy was a high school dropout. He realized pretty quickly that he had to do something extraordinary in order to become extraordinary. He started looking for people who had accomplished great things and began to *read* about them. Since then he has become wildly successful and helps millions of other people realize their greatest potentials.

In Mr. Tracy's book *Focal Point*, he "identified the areas that consumed an enormous amount of time but contributed very little to his real goals," or what Denis Waitley calls getting bogged down in "stress-relieving activities versus goal-achieving activities." By focusing on doing a small number of high-value activities he dramatically improved the quality of his life in just a few months.

Mr. Tracy says, *accepting complete responsibility for your life means that you refuse to make excuses or blame others for anything in your life that you're not happy about. You refuse, from this moment forward, to criticize others for any reason. You refuse to complain about your situation or about what has happened in the past. You eliminate all your if-onlys and what-ifs and focus instead on what you really want and where you are going.*

Do you want to look back on your life and say, "If only I would have done this differently I would have this?" I hope not. Unless you create a habit of regular maintenance in your own mind you will be one of the multitudes who look back with regret on a lifetime of missed opportunities.

You cannot afford to defer maintenance in your own life. Benjamin Franklin said, "Man can either buy his wisdom or borrow it. By buying it, he pays full price in personal time and treasure. But by borrowing it, he capitalizes on the lessons learned from the failures of others."

Don't put off expanding your mind. You will only succeed in postponing your goals and dreams from becoming reality!

58

Not Enough Yesterdays

A 1991 article in *Closer Walk* read, *In the summer of 1986, two ships collided in the Black Sea off the coast of Russia. Hundreds of passengers died as they were hurled into the icy waters below. News of the disaster was further darkened when an investigation revealed the cause of the accident. It wasn't a technology problem like radar malfunction—or even thick fog. The cause was human stubbornness. Each captain was aware of the other ship's presence nearby. Both could have steered clear, but according to news reports, neither captain wanted to give way to the other. Each was too proud to yield first. By the time they came to their senses, it was too late.*

There is something to be said for life experience. Over the years I have run into so many young people who think they know about life and choose to ignore the advice of those older and wiser. Many, certainly not all, simply have not lived along enough to be able to see the potential consequences of their decisions. They haven't had enough yesterdays in their lives to be able to look back and realize what they did right and what they did wrong.

Wisdom is realized the day people understand that they do not know what they think they know. Scientist Abraham Maslow put people in four categories when it came to figuring out how we think: unconsciously incompetent, consciously incompetent, consciously competent, and unconsciously competent.

The second tier, conscious incompetence, suggests that, though the individual does not understand how to do something, he or she recognizes the deficit. What if each of us walked around with an understanding that we do *not* know and the humility to seek out those who *do?*

Mahatma Gandhi said, "It is unwise to be too sure of one's own wisdom. It is healthy to be reminded that the strongest might weaken and the wisest might err." C. S. Lewis once said, "…A proud man is always looking down on things and people: and, of course, as long as you are looking down you cannot see something that is above you."

If each human being had a teachable point of view instead of a "know-it-all" way of thinking, we would each learn something from everyone. Back in the 1800's, Charles Spurgeon said, "Humility is to make a right estimation of oneself."

If you, like me, do not have enough yesterdays in your life to provide the wisdom that you need to help you realize where you are headed, you may want to try something I started doing years ago: seek counsel from those who have been there...from those with more yesterdays than you have. Leverage the yesterdays of many people to gain infinite insight.

This is the key from the "super successful." Orison Swett Marden was a mentor to millions. He said, "Your outlook upon life, your estimate of yourself, your estimate of your value is largely colored by your environment. Your whole career will be modified, shaped, molded by your surroundings, by the character of the people with whom you come in contact every day."

Leverage other people's experience and knowledge. Leverage their yesterdays.

59

Christmas All Year!

Is it just me or does it seem like the older we get the sooner Christmas arrives? It's interesting to me that American society focuses on giving (and getting) during only one time of the year.

The origin of Christmas is centered on the idea of personal sacrifice; that is, giving of one's self to others with no expectation of anything in return. Many years ago some societies taught their people to welcome guests into their homes by washing their feet from the dusty streets, then offer them food and a place to stay for the night without any expectation of something in return! This was a true act of humility. 2nd Corinthians, in the New Testament, says, "Each of you should give, not reluctantly or under compulsion…" I struggled with this concept for a long time. When someone did something for me, I felt compelled to try to give back. That is the law of reciprocity: a mutual exchange; rewarding kind actions; trading favors. Reciprocity as a form of social obligation calling for future acts of kindness can be seen in the Japanese word for thank you, *sumimisan*, which means "this will not end."

Dean Rieck writes, *The Rule of Reciprocity firmly states that we are all bound—even driven—to repay debts of all kinds. Someone does something for you. Then you feel obligated to repay. It's an almost automatic reaction...Cultural anthropologists Lionel Tiger and Robin Fox go so far as to claim that we live in a 'web of indebtedness' and this web is central to the human experience, responsible for the division of labor, all forms of commerce, and how society is organized into interdependent units. ... Therefore, reciprocity is a deep and powerful principle that, under the right circumstances, is all but impossible to resist.*

Why not consider giving just to give? What if we, as a society, practiced the spirit of Christmas all year? Here is what I think it would look like:

1. People would care more about giving time, talents, and treasures (money) than receiving the same.

2. People would look for ways to share instead of bargaining.

3. People would go out of their way to do more than is expected.

4. People would not give to get...they would give just to give.

5. Young people would go out of their way to share the responsibilities around their homes.

6. People would respect the elderly because of all of their accumulated wisdom.

There is a hidden benefit to giving: you will *receive* in ways you cannot imagine. Don't give to get but, when you develop the habit of giving, you open up your mind and emotions to realize blessings in your life that are beyond anything you've ever experienced.

Be a daily giver and watch your life change!

60

Protect Your Peace

When people conform to what's going on around them they adopt the attitudes and feelings of others. I heard one speaker talk about the difference between a thermostat and a thermometer. The thermostat *controls* the temperature and the thermometer *measures* it. Which one are you?

Are you in a job where your co-workers are less than ideal? Are they going to control your inner peace...are you going to be controlled by their attitudes? Do you have family that drives you crazy? In the October 2011 issue of *Forbes* magazine, Frances Cole Jones wrote, "...it doesn't matter what the 'temperature' is of the person you're dealing with—they may well be furious—but you need to remain at 70 degrees and sunny." I know first-hand that this is easier said than done. Seth Godin, one of my favorite writers and thinkers, says, "...a thermometer is great for identifying when something is broken after the fact while a thermostat does its best job to regulate temperature to stay in sync with its environment. Thermostats are leaders while thermometers are just squeaky wheels."

I'm sure you have seen people panic because *other* people panic. The same goes for some who are afraid of things like swimming in deep water, snakes, speaking in public, etc. Many of those fears are learned. They are passed down from one person to another. It's time to break that chain.

The temptation is to give in to those outside influences that can change your mood, outlook on life, and, frankly, your *mission* in life. The distraction of other people's agendas, habits, attitudes, and lifestyles should not keep you from maintaining a balance in your own life. The tendency to adopt the attitudes of those around you can be enormous. Carry your own peace with you. Do not let the lack of planning by other people create an emergency in your life.

How can you do this? First, written daily, monthly, and annual goals are essential to maintain inner balance. Second, post these goals where you can see them every day. You will find, in time, that when circumstances and situations threaten to "rock your boat" your written goals will keep your feet firmly planted.

Be a thermostat and protect your inner peace!

61

Reacting to Yesterday

A while back, I had an a-ha moment as I was watching the Oprah Winfrey Network. Before I tell you what I saw and heard, travel back with me to about 1968.

In 1968, when I was less than two years old, I slipped on the landing of our stairs in our row home in Lakeland, Maryland. I fell all the way down the twelve or so steps to the bottom. I remember it as if it happened yesterday. I remember that I could not stop my fall no matter how much I tried. For years and years I have been afraid of heights. Could the fall in 1968 have something to do with that fear? It's as if I made a decision, unconsciously, to exercise as much control over my own life as possible so I won't "fall" again.

Fast-forward to 2011 when I was watching the Oprah Winfrey Network and heard something that brought incredible clarity to me. A doctor on the show said that people who are afraid of heights have a fear of being "out of control" of their surroundings. That is, they feel most secure when they can control what's happening around them and to them. They have a fear of "letting go" in order to be free. They're afraid of trusting anyone or anything. That got me thinking, not only about my life, but about the thousands of people with whom I've worked over the years.

How many people reading this book have been stuck in the rut of yesterday because of something that happened in the past? How many of us have placed our futures in the hands of our past difficulties, stereotypes, bad relationships, past failures, and struggles? How many live so much in the past that we find it difficult to grab hold of new ventures and new opportunities?

That show forced me to find a rock-climbing wall and GO FOR IT! Will it be scary? Yes! But, if I teach that we have to try to explode from our fears, then I have to be first in line to overcome mine.

We each have to decide to face what has, maybe unconsciously, been holding us back. Take a moment or two to look back in order to move forward. The time has come to look through your history and use those events that were meant to destroy you or slow you down to help you catapult from an ordinary life to an *extraordinary* life. Diagnose the situations in your past that may have stopped you in your tracks and see if they are still stumbling blocks. My fear of heights has not destroyed me but it has kept me from enjoying certain sights. How about you? What is keeping you from enjoying a life that is just beyond your reach? Climb your wall! Overcome that pain of the past, choose to look beyond yesterday, and run toward a brighter tomorrow!

62

Is It Possible?

As a kid I was always amazed by magicians. The way they were able to make me believe that their tricks were real was amazing. I saw magicians walking through walls and catching bullets in their teeth. I knew what I was seeing was not real but I also knew what I saw with my own eyes. That started me on the path of questioning which things I saw with my own eyes were real and which were not.

What have we, as a society, placed in our minds that seems to be "real?" For many years, much of America considered people of African descent to be something less than human. Was that reality? Of course not. There are many in America who believe that those who lack a college education or who live in a certain part of town can't make it big-time in life. Is that reality? Of course not! There are many who assume that "what is will always be." Is this reality? Of course not! When we adopted our children from Russia and Belarus we were told not to give them anything cold (including ice cream) until they were five or six years old. I guess they thought it would make them sick. Was that a reality for us as parents? Of course not! We gave them ice cream as soon as possible and they didn't get sick. Amazing! There are many who believe that those in prisons and jails are beyond help and cannot be "rewired." I disagree!

Today, I'd like you to question your "reality" and the societal "norms" that are in existence today. Is it possible for you to overcome obstacles in your past? Of course! Is it possible to overcome your lack of information about certain subjects that interest you? Of course! Is it possible to step beyond the expectations of people around you that continue to keep you in a mental "box?" Of course!!

Your belief system has more power than you can imagine! It can enable you to look discouragement in the eye and spit in it. *The words you CHOOSE TO SPEAK have tremendous power to mold your own possibilities!* What if you were able to track the words you use and how your language connects to your potential? You would be amazed by the implications! Magicians use words and misdirection to trick us into believing what we are seeing on their stage. What if we were intentional about our words and our direction? It would alter our possibilities. Stop being an echo. Be an original! Your belief system can pull you toward becoming the ideal *you*. Is it possible? Of course!

63

Thimble Thinking

A Thimble is a tiny, hard, pitted cup worn for protection on the finger when sewing. Many people have just enough goals and dreams to fill a thimble. I keep one on my desk or (sometimes) in my pocket to remind me not to think small. Many people continue to think small because they surround themselves with people who think small. I could tell you stories about this all day.

Thimble thinking is not for you. David J. Schwartz, in *The Magic of Thinking Big*, wrote, *Think you are weak, think you lack what it takes, think you will lose, think you are second class—think this way and you are doomed to mediocrity…Believe it can be done. When you believe something can be done, really believe, your mind will find the ways to do it. Believing a solution paves the way to solution.*

You are better than a thimble thinker. Decide to ignore the thimble thinkers around you. Avoid hanging around those who shoot down your dreams and goals. Choose to, as Stephen Covey said, live out your imagination and not your history: *The key is not to prioritize what's on your schedule, but to schedule your priorities.*

That last piece of advice is critical to your success. Life has a way of pushing aside our goals and dreams so much that many people wake up when they're old only to find out that it is too late. Don't let this happen to you. Take the limitations off of your possibilities!!

64

More Important
Than Your Fears

For decades I've had certain fears that still take effort to over-come. One of them is the fear of public speaking. In fact, it can be more like a terror. If I knew I had to speak, the anticipation made me sick to my stomach. Finally, someone taught me that fears can be overcome simply by doing the dreaded activity over and over. Hiding from my fears only makes them stronger.

We each have a choice to see the obvious or to see the pos-sibilities. In ancient times people used scales to measure grain, fish, and other items for purposes of transacting business. On one side of the scale are your fears and on the other side of the scale are your hopes and dreams. The more you feed your fear the "heavier" it gets as it takes you farther from your hopes and dreams. The uncertainty of what you cannot see can keep you from taking a leap of faith.

James Allen said, "The greatest achievement was at first and for a time a dream. The oak sleeps in the acorn; the bird waits in the egg; and in the highest vision of the soul a waking angel stirs. Dreams are the seedlings of realities."

I was made fun of in school because I had a severe speech difficulty. When teachers called on me I shrugged my shoulders even though I knew the answer. I was terrified to speak up and risk being laughed at by my peers.

Dale Carnegie said, "Inaction breeds doubt and fear. Action breeds confidence and courage. If you want to conquer fear, do not sit home and think about it. Go out and get busy."

I took Mr. Carnegie's advice in several areas of my life and, although I still struggle with some fears, I am impacting more people than I ever thought possible. You can do the same. What you think is impossible...isn't! What you think you cannot over-come...you can! The old Japanese proverb that says "Fear is only as deep as the mind allows" reminds me that, for many years, my mind kept me from reaching out to the thousands of people who need encouragement and inspiration. One of my mentors, Jordan Adler, said, "Make your dreams more important than your fears." So, with the help of lots of books by people who have realized great accomplishments, I began a journey to make a difference.

What or who is most important in your life? Are your fears bigger than your dreams? Is your capacity smaller than your dreams? You have more in you than you realize. Leverage your experiences, stand on your fear, kick aside your doubt, and impose upon yourself a life where fear is in the back seat instead of behind the wheel.

65

What Does
It Look Like?

Most people have no idea where they want to be in their lives in one year, five years, or even ten years. Imagine if a home builder, upon starting a project, had no idea what it would look like when he finished. In fact, home builders work backwards! Builders get a blueprint of the final product then work to make that blueprint a reality. What if you were a baker? Your final product is an apple pie. The exact ingredients you choose to use will enable you to create the final product: the apple pie.

Isn't it a better idea to plan your life than to just let life happen? The first thing you should do is to write down what you want your life to look like in 1 year...5 years...and 10 years.

Once that is completed it is essential to keep that document in front of you *all the time*. The next step is to write down *why* you wish to accomplish these 1, 5, and 10-year goals. *This is crucial!* If you don't write down *why* you want these things discouragement will keep you from achieving them.

Early in his career, actor Jim Carrey wrote himself a $10 Million check for "acting services rendered." He placed this check in his wallet to remind him of his potential and a reminder never to give up. The day came when he was able to cash that check when a company paid him $10 Million for acting in a movie.

When my wife and I married in 1988 we planned on having children "the old fashioned way." After nine years of infertility we started adopting children from overseas. First, we adopted two children and then one more. Our family was complete. We decided, *in writing,* to start helping other families adopt and to take trips overseas to deliver toys and medicines to orphanages in Russia. On our first trip, in the orphanage where two of our children had lived, I was introduced to Sergie. I sat down on the floor to play with him and introduced myself as John. The doctor who was sitting across the room said "nyet...nyet...*Daddy.*" We eventually adopted Sergie and took him home. In our efforts to help other families we heard of two little girls in Belarus. We adopted *them.* Here's the best part: Our fifth child, one of the two who came from Belarus, was stricken with cancer shortly after we adopted her. She was five years old at the time. She beat it. The cancer came back in 2011 when she was nine. So far she has beaten it again. *What if we hadn't written down our life plan?* Other people would not have been impacted and our daughter, Juliana, would have died a horrible death in Belarus.

Jim Rohn once said, "If you don't design your own life plan, chances are you'll fall into someone else's plan. Guess what they have planned for you? NOT MUCH!"

Now that the description of your ideal life is written down, write down, in great detail, *how* you are going to realize those 1, 5, and 10-year goals. Remember the home builder and the baker? Once they understand *what* they're trying to accomplish they have to accumulate the means (the *how*) to make it a reality. So it is with your life. You have more control than you realize!

Finally, now that you have written it all down, what does your new life look like?

Remember, NOTHING IS IMPOSSIBLE!

66

The Paths

A few years ago my wife and I bought a six-and-a-half acre piece of ground on the Maryland/Pennsylvania line. Soon thereafter we built our home. Most of the property was wooded with poison ivy and briers as well as mature trees. The briars and weeds were so thick our kids couldn't play on a couple acres of the land so I made a decision. I decided to create a few paths through the wooded areas. It was HARD WORK! Mowing down thorns, getting stuck a few times, cutting down obstructions, and encountering poison ivy made the creation of the paths slower than I expected. For several months (off and on) I would work on the paths so our kids could maximize the land that we purchased. One day, my paths all met! I felt like it was a personal breakthrough. Now our kids, my wife, and anyone else can walk through a few acres of paths and not have to worry about getting stuck by briers or getting poison ivy. Why am I telling this story? The paths don't just stay clear by themselves. Every couple of weeks I have to go through them with trimmers and weed killer to keep them open and clear.

What does this have to do with you? There are people who have cleared paths for YOU to walk on and enjoy the fruits of their labors. They paid the price so that others can bypass most of the difficulties they had to endure. The key is to locate these people and read about what they learned so they can help you in your life. It's like "standing on the shoulders of giants." This is what I have done for many years. I stand upon the shoulders of John C. Maxwell, Mark Sanborn, Stephen Covey, Brian Tracy, Denis Waitley, Charlie "Tremendous" Jones, Seth Godin, Tom Peters, Napoleon Hill, Jim Rohn, Anthony Robbins, Peter Drucker, Marcus Buckingham, Og Mandino, and many more. By the way, ALL these people stood on the shoulders of other giants to reach their goals and dreams.

Brian Tracy said, "If you could find out what the most successful people did in any area and then you did the same thing over and over, you'd eventually get the same result they do."

Think about these pioneers who have cleared the way for you to find out the secrets of realizing your goals and dreams. It is their gift to you! They paid the price, endured the pain, and left a path for you to follow. Choose to master what you need to know to open paths for you and for others to enjoy!

67

The Shoelace

I was with Arthur, a friend I have known my entire life when a mutual friend of ours, John, almost twenty years older than Arthur, approached. John had a stroke a couple years ago and hadn't noticed that his shoelace was untied. Arthur got down on one knee and tied John's shoelace. I said something like, "Now this shows the real character of a man." Arthur hadn't hesitated. He saw someone in need and did something about it. He showed his love for John through his actions.

Love is very delicate. True love goes beyond words. True love is defined by an ancient passage from 1st Corinthians, paraphrased here by Eugene H. Peterson, that says, "Love never gives up. Love cares more for others than for self. Love doesn't want what it doesn't have. Love doesn't strut, doesn't have a swelled head, doesn't force itself on others, isn't always 'me first', doesn't fly off the handle, doesn't keep score of the sins of others, doesn't revel when others grovel, takes pleasure in the flowering of truth, puts up with anything, always looks for the best, never looks back, but keeps going to the end."

In December 2012 I listened as someone expressed their love for someone, but their actions were just the opposite of true love. C.S. Lewis wrote, *Do not waste your time bothering whether you 'love' your neighbor; act as if you did. As soon as we do this, we find one of the great secrets. When you are behaving as if you loved someone, you will presently come to love him. If you do him a good turn, you will find yourself disliking him less.*

Do your actions match your words? Do you say, "I Love you" yet your actions fail to match the ancient verses of 1st Corinthians? Love is not about you. It's always about other people. Begin today. Look for ways to do good things for people with no expectation of recognition or anything in return, but be cautious of those who say they love but lack actions to match their words.

Go ahead…tie someone's shoelace today!

– B L O C K –

68

"Be the Change"

Some people wish the world was a better place, or they wish society was this way or that way, or they wish they could achieve something amazing in life. These people live in *Wish Land*, a state of mind in which people see change as a wish and not a possibility. I remember when President Ronald Reagan suggested that the Soviet Union would one day be no more. He was able to move past his Wish Land to a state of mind in which he helped to facilitate a situation, environment, and dialogue that helped create an atmosphere where the peoples of the Soviet Union could choose their own leaders and give birth to a family of new nations.

Those who move past a Wish Land mentality become *Influentials* in their own culture and, many times, in other cultures as well. Ed Keller and Jon Berry wrote a book called *The Influencials* in which they highlight the characteristics of those who become Influentials. If you seek to become an Influential in your own life then consider emulating some of the habits that Keller and Berry identified:

- They attend community meetings.
- They serve on committees.
- They volunteer even though they live busy lives.
- They READ!!!
- They have ties to a larger number of groups than the average person.
- They are people to whom others look for advice.
- They have active minds and a restless intellect.
- They are determined to overcome personal obstacles.
- They believe change is a good thing.
- They are clear-headed about their priorities.
- They use multiple sources for information.
- Again, they READ...A LOT!!

If you wish to see change in your own life then there needs to be a change in the way you think about yourself. Earl Nightingale, in his classic recording *The Strangest Secret,* points out that *conformity* is one of the greatest dangers in American Society. He defines conformity as "people acting like everyone else, without knowing why or without knowing where they are going." If we blindly conform to the habits, words, and actions of those who "don't have a clue" where they are heading, the end result for us is obvious.

You CAN change! It begins with the realization that you have the *capacity* to do great things in your life, that you will make the *daily* changes to create an environment that will propel you toward your goals and dreams, and you will *avoid* those people who do not believe in your potential. Do not assume that only "special" people can create the lifestyle they wish to live. If you believe that you were born for greatness, if you develop right habits, and if you feed your mind and spirit the material that you need to excel, then no one can stop you...no one!

You can be the one who is a catalyst for your entire household, neighborhood, city, state, and country. **It starts with YOU!** BE THE CHANGE!

About the Author

John Carver grew up in Baltimore, Maryland. His business career began in 1988 when he got into the insurance industry. In 1998, John and his wife, Tammy, adopted six children from Russia and Belarus.

John Carver believes in the potential in every human being. He believes that each of us has gifts and talents that have not been realized; that each human being is uniquely qualified to be extraordinary. Most people, however, do not know what it takes to reach that level of excellence in their own lives. The Carver Group opens minds to their potential and helps people achieve their goals and dreams.

John helps show thousands of people every week what it takes to overcome difficulties and obstructions in order to go from mediocrity to excellence. His teachings are ancient as well as new. John can bring instant direction to the American public in ways they haven't experienced in their lives. In today's economy America needs the words and experience of John Carver.

Listen to John's half-hour daily radio/Internet show at http://www.BlogTalkRadio.com/TheJohnCarverShow and visit his website at www.JohnWCarver.com